Coping with

SCHIZOPHRENIA

Evelyn B. Kelly, Ph.D.

The Rosen Publishing Group, Inc.
New York

Published in 2001 by The Rosen Publishing Group, Inc.
29 East 21st Street, New York, NY 10010

First Edition

Image on page 26 © SuperStock.

Library of Congress Cataloging-in-Publication Data

Kelly, Evelyn B.
    Coping with schizophrenia / Evelyn B. Kelly—1st ed.
    p. cm.
  Includes bibliographical references and index.
  ISBN: 978-1-4358-8632-2
    1. Schizophrenia—Juvenile literature. 2. Schizophrenics—Family relationships—Juvenile literature. [1. Schizophrenia. 2. Mental illness.] I. Title.
  RC514 .K36 2000
616.89'82—dc21
                                                        00-009848

Manufactured in the United States of America

About the Author

Evelyn B. Kelly, Ph.D., is a writer, educator, and community activist living in Ocala, Florida. She has written seven books and 300 articles on various topics. As a medical writer, she specializes in genetic disorders and disorders of the nervous system. She is a professor of education at Saint Leo University in Florida and has worked with students of all ages for twenty years.

Acknowledgments

The author expresses her heartfelt thanks to the Marion County, Florida, chapter of the National Alliance for the Mentally Ill (NAMI). She also wishes to thank the many people who talked with her and the friends she met on-line who provided valuable information about their experiences.

Contents

Introduction

Dear Dr. Martinez,

My family and I need help. A friend of mine suggested I write to you because we are too embarrassed to talk with anyone face-to-face and let anyone know.

It's my older brother Jason. At one time Jason was the greatest. He was a good student in high school, and he was so much fun to be around and hang out with. Last year, though, he went off to college on a drama scholarship and he suddenly changed. Now he's like a person we don't even know. He quit the drama club and we think he may not even be going to classes.

Jason was always a neat freak about his personal appearance, a real preppy, but now he looks awful and acts strange. He always looks like he hasn't showered in a week, maybe two. He also told his roommate he hears Mom's voice telling him to do things. I've heard that crazy people hear voices. We are really worried.

My friend, the one who told me to write to you, said it sounds like schizophrenia, but I don't know anything about it and neither does my family. Another friend told me it was a split personality disorder, when the person acts evil and then really nice and sweet—sort of like Dr. Jekyll and Mr. Hyde.

Yesterday, we received a letter from his roommate, Corey, who described some of Jason's unusual behavior. Corey said he was studying when all of a sudden

1

Jason jumped up and screamed that there were snakes under his bed. Corey said that at first he thought Jason was just fooling around, but then Jason started crying and yelling "Help me!" really loud. Now, Corey wants to move out.

At first, we thought Jason was just doing all of this weird stuff to get our attention because he missed living at home with us, but even though we have started to call him every night and we visit him every weekend, Jason seems to be getting worse. Last week, I was up visiting. We were walking to the cafeteria for lunch, and Jason started telling me that he thought he was King Lear, you know, from Shakespeare's play. I tried to tell him that King Lear is a fictitious character, and not real, but Jason got really mad at me and told me to go home and leave him alone.

What is schizophrenia? Please help us, Dr. Martinez. We are so worried.

Lisa

Lisa wrote this letter to Dr. Martinez, a clinical psychologist in her hometown who speaks to groups about mental illness. Dr. Martinez is an advocate for mental health and specializes in cases of people who have schizophrenia. Like Lisa, you may not have ever heard of schizophrenia (pronounced *skit-se-FRE-nee-uh*). You might think that Jason is messed up, making bad decisions, and acting crazy. However, Jason is not crazy or insane—he is ill. Just like someone who is ill because he or she has cancer, Jason is ill because he has schizophrenia.

This book will provide you with information about schizophrenia. It is only an introduction and is not a substitute for your doctor or mental health professional. Instead, it has been written to help you and your family learn about schizophrenia: its symptoms, the behavioral changes it causes, and the process of diagnosing and treating it. You might think of this as a guidebook of information to point you in the right direction and help clear up some of the confusion that surrounds this illness. This is why the book discusses a lot of practical coping skills as well as some of the information science has revealed about schizophrenia.

Also discussed are the several stages a family will move through if a member has this illness: from the time the family sees early signs of schizophrenia, such as behavior changes, to diagnosis and possible treatments. There is also a section that explains what it is like to have schizophrenia and suggests coping strategies for those with the disease.

This book is designed to:

⇔ Teach you about the disease

⇔ Show that schizophrenia is not preventable or caused by anyone

⇔ Explain its symptoms, diagnosis, and treatment

⇔ Illustrate how to communicate with medical professionals and family

The first step in coping with schizophrenia is understanding it. When dealing with schizophrenia, whether it is because you, a friend, or a family member has the illness, knowledge is power. Chapter 1 defines schizophrenia and discusses the main types as well as some related conditions.

Schizophrenia is a disease that may appear in many forms. Recognizing the symptoms may not be as easy as you think. The causes of schizophrenia are also very questionable.

Doctors have some impressive research and theories about the disease, but these are not definite or completely developed. The reality of the disease—that there is not exact information on schizophrenia—is also discussed in chapter 1.

Chapter 2 discusses the early warning signs and symptoms of the illness. Knowing these will enable you and your family to have beneficial sessions with the various health professionals that you may come in contact with. Chapter 3 is about communication, offering some practical ideas on learning how to communicate effectively.

Diagnosis of schizophrenia is by exclusion; this means many things must be ruled out before a complete diagnosis can be made. Chapter 4 discusses the elements of diagnosis and points out conditions that mimic schizophrenia. How to find a doctor and health team is also included in this chapter so that you can find the best people to help you or your family member.

Chapter 5 features important discussions for anyone who knows a person with schizophrenia, such as what it is like to have schizophrenia, how people who have it feel during an episode, and what they think about the illness. Several people who are dealing with the condition talk about their experiences.

Chapter 6 outlines treatments and includes biological treatments, such as medication, and nonbiological treatments, such as psychotherapy. Chapter 7, on the other hand, presents the history of mental illness. In this chapter, you will meet some of the major players in the development of understanding about schizophrenia.

Chapter 8 is a technical section that will discuss the detailed anatomy of the brain, similar to what you may have learned in biology. A discussion of brain chemistry is also presented, to show the importance of biochemical workings such as neurotransmitters. In this chapter, you will also learn about some of the theories of inheritance, which show that mental illness may be passed from generation to generation.

Chapter 9 focuses on how schizophrenia affects families and gives detailed suggestions on how family members can cope with this disease.

How do you become an advocate and do something to help the cause of mental health? Chapter 10 focuses on becoming an advocate, discusses self-help groups like the National Alliance for the Mentally Ill (NAMI), and considers what you can do to help. This chapter also outlines challenges for the twenty-first century.

Schizophrenia affects 2.2 million Americans, and it often strikes people between the ages of sixteen and twenty-five—just when life should be most exciting. While there is no cure at present, schizophrenia is treatable. However, it is sometimes difficult to get accurate and reliable information about schizophrenia. The goal of this book is to provide information that will assist you in learning about and coping with schizophrenia.

What Is Schizophrenia?

It may be that you think you already know what schizophrenia is: You think that schizophrenics are the people you see walking down the street talking to themselves, yelling at people, who may even be dangerous because they can no longer distinguish right from wrong. This perception may be due to what we read about or see in the movies and on television, possibly even what we hear on the news. But this description of a schizophrenic is not accurate—it is an example of how many misconceptions there are about schizophrenics. According to *Mental Health: A Report of the Surgeon General,* this type of perception of mental illness is the largest obstacle in making progress. In reality, little violence is associated with schizophrenia.

The Disease

Everyone has heard the word "schizophrenia." There is even a popular term, used when someone acts strange; he or she is described as being "schizo." But schizophrenia is a mental illness, a real disease that is chronic and severe. New research has shown that the disorder is caused by changes in brain chemistry.

As defined by *Webster's New World Dictionary of the American Language,* schizophrenia is "a major mental disorder of unknown cause typically characterized by a separation between the thought processes and the emotions; a distortion of reality accompanied by delusions and hallucinations, a fragmentation of the personality, motor disturbances, bizarre behavior, etc., often with no loss of basic intelligence functions." Although this definition is a mouthful, it certainly shows the disease is complex. No definition, however, is really adequate in defining schizophrenia because it is a disease of the brain, and the brain is incredibly complex.

Schizophrenia is not an infectious disease such as measles or the flu, nor is it a disease similar to cancer or lung disease. Schizophrenia is a disease that comes from the brain. Unlike food poisoning, there are no bacteria that cause it; unlike AIDS, it is not spread by a virus. To date, no one has devised a test that says yes, you have schizophrenia.

Even though schizophrenia is a mental illness, it is being referred to more often as a neurobiological disorder, or NBD. The term has not caught on yet, but as knowledge and information about mental illness increase, it will become more widespread. You can help by referring to schizophrenia as an NBD when you are explaining it to your friends.

In order to understand and be able to explain schizophrenia, there are some things you need to know. Living with a person with schizophrenia can be a nightmare and much like a roller-coaster ride. You can help yourself by becoming informed.

What Is an NBD?

Schizophrenia is a neurobiological disease, or NBD. An NBD is a condition where an individual cannot control his or her thoughts. This happens not only in schizophrenia but also in major depression, manic or bipolar depression, panic disorder, and obsessive-compulsive disorder. The person may have hallucinations, which are distortions of the senses due to the brain's inability to interpret and respond to incoming information. Hallucinations cause people to hear or see things that are not there. About three-fourths of people with schizophrenia hear voices during their illness. These are called auditory hallucinations. Sometimes the voices are complimentary, reassuring, or neutral. Sometimes they are threatening, frightening, or commanding.

Other sensory hallucinations are rarer: olfactory (persistent sense of an unpleasant smell), gustatory (the presence of bad tastes), somatic (a feeling of persistent pain), or visual (seeing terrifying things like dead people or animals). While these sensory hallucinations may not be as persistent as the auditory ones, they are just as terrifying. The main feature of schizophrenia is a loss of touch with reality, which is why schizophrenics' behavior often seems inappropriate. They may laugh at the wrong time or become very excited about nothing. At other times, they may be completely rational and seem fine.

Subtypes of Schizophrenia

People with schizophrenia may display a wide variety of behaviors. While some schizophrenic behavior may differ only slightly from what is considered normal, other schizophrenic behavior can be extremely unusual. From the various behavior patterns that schizophrenics display, the following four kinds of schizophrenia have been defined.

Undifferentiated Type
The most prevalent sign of the undifferentiated type is a significant reduction of outside interests and relationships. The

person's emotions may lack depth, and he or she may show an absence of mental activity. The person withdraws to simple forms of behavior.

Hebephrenic Type

Most often, disorganized behavior is the key symptom of the hebephrenic type. "Hebe" comes from the name of the goddess of youth in Greek mythology. The hebephrenic person displays childish or bizarre behavior and may have delusions, which are false beliefs, or hallucinations. Bizarre types of behavior may involve things like playing with paper dolls.

Catatonic Type

The catatonic type has very unusual motor behavior. The person may not move or talk for long periods of time and may assume a pose much like a statue. These periods of inactivity may alternate with periods of excitement. A person's behavior tends to be impulsive and unpredictable.

Paranoid Type

The paranoid type is characterized by delusions of grandeur, illogical thinking, and hallucinations. Sometimes people may feel others are after them or plotting against them.

It is important to remember that these types are not exclusive and some schizophrenics may show a mixture. There may be some cases that defy classification. Some may even have a mixture of symptoms, combining certain symptoms of schizophrenia with some symptoms of other types of psychosis.

A manual called the *Diagnostic and Statistical Manual of Mental Disorders,* or *DSM,* describes the specific types and symptoms of mental disorders. There are similar disorders that do not meet the criteria of schizophrenia. Schizoaffective disorders, for example, exhibit features of both schizophrenia and affective disorders. Affective symptoms are mania, depression, and irritability. These are seen equally in schizophrenia.

Psychosis NOS, or "not otherwise specified," is when people have schizophrenic-like illnesses but do not fit any defined categories. Psychosis NOS may be used as a temporary category for people who definitely have a disorder but need a more precise diagnosis.

Finally, there is schizotypal personality disorder. People who fall into this category may have mild schizophrenia. These are people whose behavior may be labeled "eccentric." They may have poor social skills or unusual emotional responses.

What Is an Episode?

When a person has an attack of schizophrenia, the term to describe this period of time is "episode." Some people may have only one episode, while others have several or multiple episodes over a period of years. Others may be ill all of the time or for the rest of their lives.

What causes the behavior of a normal person to change? The specific cause is not known. The explanation currently recognized by scientists is based on brain chemicals called neurotransmitters—molecules that spur electrical signals of the brain into movement. How, when, and why neurotransmission begins to change and creates schizophrenia are subjects of intense scientific investigation.

Schizophrenia is found everywhere, cutting across all races, cultures, and social classes. It affects 1 in 100 people worldwide. Let's say your high school has 2,000 students—that means there would probably be twenty people who may be affected by schizophrenia in some way. A point that needs to be emphasized is that people with an NBD are not "crazy" or "nuts." Your friends may use these terms, but now that you are learning the facts, it is your responsibility to correct misconceptions about schizophrenia.

Can Children Develop Schizophrenia?

The symptoms that children with schizophrenia develop are somewhat like those of adults with the disease, except that the subjects of their hallucinations are related to their age experience. A child may have hallucinations involving pets or toys. A recurring theme is monsters. Sometimes it is difficult to establish the line between schizophrenic symptoms, dreams, and normal childhood imagination.

Onset of the disease occurs in childhood in only about 2 percent of cases, and thus a schizophrenic before age five is exceedingly rare. The condition may be confused with autism, hyperactivity, mental retardation, or other behavior problems. At one time, general terms such as "school phobia" were used, but recently, the American Psychiatric Association deleted childhood schizophrenia from its official listing of illnesses, changing it to a general "childhood-onset pervasive development disorder."

Males Versus Females

Although more males are affected than females in childhood, looking at statistics of teens and adults, one might assume males and females are at equal risk for the condition. However, the time the disease strikes is very different in men and women. Generally, the onset is two to three years earlier in men. Men also seem to have more severe cases and do not respond as well to medication. There is speculation that the female hormone estrogen may have an antipsychotic effect.

Can Schizophrenia Begin After Age Forty?

Schizophrenia that begins at a later age is called late-onset. Most research that pertains to late-onset has been done in Europe, as Americans have shown little interest in the problem. Late-onset is more common among females, and it tends to be chronic, with less hope for recovery.

What Causes Schizophrenia?

We do not have the precise answer, but some of the pieces are becoming clearer. Areas of study include the following, and as they are discussed, be sure to pay attention to how many different theories there are in existence. The many theories show that schizophrenia is still very much a mystery.

Biochemistry

People with schizophrenia appear to have a neurochemical imbalance. A chemical imbalance interferes with a person's ability to think clearly and to manage emotions. The person has major problems making decisions and relating to others. Modern medications, such as lithium, target imbalanced neurotransmitters and try to balance them out so that the person can process thoughts clearly.

Cerebral Blood Flow

With modern brain imaging techniques called PET scans, researchers have identified areas of the brain that are activated when processing information. Studies indicate people with schizophrenia have some difficulty in processing information in specific areas of their brains.

Molecular Biology and Genetic Predisposition

Molecular biologists focus on irregular patterns of certain brain cells that could have formed before birth and may be triggered at a later age. Similarly, genetic predisposition means that there is a hereditary gene for schizophrenia, and research is beginning to reflect that it does exist. Schizophrenia does appear more regularly in some families, but it also appears in families with no history of the illness. Although several chromosomes are suspected, their definite locations have yet to be identified.

Stress and Drug Abuse

Although stress and drug abuse do not cause schizophrenia, both make the symptoms worse when the illness is already present. However, many times both are a chronic problem for schizophrenics. Therefore, not only do they have a mental illness to cope with but they might have an addiction or a very unhealthy level of stress.

Virus Hypothesis and Nutritional Theories

The virus hypothesis is an area of study in which researchers believe a slow-acting virus may be the cause of schizophrenia. Viruses are very sneaky, and they often cause a host of infections. If schizophrenia is a virus, it would be even more complex than initially thought, and the possibility of a cure would be much farther away.

Nutritional theories are a gray area of study because, although proper nutrition is important, there is little proof that lack of vitamins has any direct link to schizophrenia. It has been found, however, that megavitamins, or high doses of a certain vitamin, can help make symptoms less intense.

Dr. Nancy Andreasen, in her book *The Broken Brain: The Biological Revolution in Psychiatry*, explains that schizophrenia is like a mosaic, a multifaceted illness that "includes changes in the chemistry of the brain, changes in the structure of the brain, and genetic factors. Viral factors and head injuries may also play a role. Finally, schizophrenia is probably a group of related diseases, some of which are caused by one factor and some by another." As research becomes more efficient and technologically advanced, expect to hear more about the multifaceted umbrella of schizophrenia.

What Schizophrenia Is Not

Loads of misinformation exists about schizophrenia. The term literally means "split mind." The use of the term has caused a lot of confusion. Popular culture has defined split mind as a person with dual personalities, but the term actually refers to all the things that make up an integrated human personality, such as logical thinking, feeling, and perception.

Another piece of misinformation is that schizophrenia is an emotional disturbance. Most people assume that, as a child, the schizophrenic suffered child abuse, trauma, or some other horrible event that caused the condition. This is not true. Other people assume that the disorder is a result of bad parenting or a lack of love. This is also not true. The events of one's life do not cause the disease.

Confusion with Other Conditions

Other conditions are usually associated with schizophrenia, but these conditions are very distinct and are not related in any way.

Facts About Schizophrenia

- Schizophrenia is strictly a human disease. Animals do not have the condition.

- In addition to the four subtypes, researchers are now proposing a multidimensional model in which the types interact.

- In the last two decades, powerful imaging techniques have been developed in which activity of the brain is photographed. This may lead to the discovery of the parts of the brain that cause schizophrenia.

- Brain-imaging technology shows that schizophrenia is an organic brain disorder, just like multiple sclerosis, Parkinson's disease, or Alzheimer's disease.

- Some speculate that the female hormone estrogen may affect the parts of the brain that cause schizophrenia.

- Schizophrenia is a disorder with specific symptoms caused by physical and chemical changes in the brain.

- The illness affects people in the prime of their lives—between the ages of sixteen and twenty-five.

It is important that you know about these conditions because then you can distinguish between schizophrenia and other mental illnesses. Remember, knowledge is power.

Mental Retardation

Mental retardation is an impairment of learning ability, most often measured by IQ, or Intelligence Quotient, tests. Occasionally, a person with schizophrenia may also be mentally retarded, but the conditions are independent and the combination of the two happens only by chance.

Manic-Depression and Borderline Personality

Only one-half as prevalent as schizophrenia, manic-depressive psychosis is characterized by wide mood swings, whereas people who have borderline personality disorder may be unstable in their relationships and behavior. They may be impulsive and unpredictable, and may be prone to temper tantrums and emotional outbursts.

Brief Psychotic Illness and Drug Psychosis

Brief psychotic illness disorders develop because of extreme stress. A war experience or isolation with little stimulation might cause a temporary episode. The illness does not persist and usually clears up within one to six months. Drug psychosis, or the use of street drugs such as LSD, is easily confused with schizophrenia. When under the influence of these drugs, the person often experiences hallucinations and his or her behavior looks inappropriate to everyone else. Also, certain prescription drugs may mimic psychosis. You may not be aware that things like bug spray may cause psychotic-like symptoms in some people.

Myths and Facts About Schizophrenia

Myths

- Schizophrenics have split personalities.

- Schizophrenics are always violent.

- Drug and alcohol abuse cause schizophrenia.

- A bad childhood and an unsupportive family cause schizophrenia.

- Schizophrenia is an emotional disturbance caused by abuse, trauma, or other mistreatment.

Facts

- Schizophrenics have one personality.

- Schizophrenics are rarely violent.

- Drugs and alcohol make symptoms worse, but they do not cause the illness.

- Schizophrenia is a neurobiological disease, a disease of the brain, and it is not caused by a person's family.

- Schizophrenia can distort the senses, so that a person cannot tell what is real and not real.

- Early diagnosis and treatment can improve the possibilities for normal life functions.

Early Warning Signs and Symptoms

Jane was nineteen when her doctor recommended she spend some time in a mental health clinic. In the past, she had been a smart and articulate student, but for the past year she had barely left the house and now she was failing her senior year of high school.

On the day of her arrival at the clinic, she told the examining physician that she really did not know why she was there. When the doctor tried to ask her something, she would just sit there and play with the frayed edges of her wool sweater. Suddenly, with a straight face, she said, "It all happened a year ago. The president put truth serum in my drinking water. Now I can hear people telling me their sins."

She giggled and dropped her head so her black curls covered her face. "I know what your sins are."

When she looked up again her face was very calm. It was over. She would not talk anymore.

Healthy Versus Unhealthy

In a healthy person, the brain receives stimuli and processes the information in a logical response. For example, someone hands you a gift for your birthday, you take it, and you give the logical acknowledgment of "thank you." Or maybe you are late to school, but because you are aware of the rules you know what will happen before you get there. The logical consequence of being late is getting a warning or receiving detention.

One of the hallmarks of schizophrenia is the inability to sort stimuli and respond appropriately. Instead, because of interruptions in the nerve transmissions, signals are mixed up and the future consequences of one's actions are poorly understood.

Early Signs

Just like other diseases, schizophrenia has signs and symptoms. They may not be spots like measles or high fever and cough like influenza, but they are real symptoms. However, they are not the same for everyone.

A general symptom that always happens is a change in personality and ability. It is obvious that the person is not the same. Most often, the changes are observed by family, friends, or teachers. Changes in academic or work activities, social relationships, and personal hygiene are also warning signs of schizophrenia.

Areas of Change

A personality change is a key to recognizing schizophrenia. At first these changes may be minor and no one may even be able to see them. Then over time, the change will become more drastic, and family, friends, classmates, teachers, or even coworkers will begin to notice. The sufferer will exhibit moodiness and withdraw from the social world. The person will have little interest in his or her previous activities and hobbies, a loss or lack of emotion, and little to no motivation. An outgoing, friendly person may become quiet, withdrawn, and moody.

Thought disorder is probably the most noticeable change. The person will not think clearly and rationally. Thoughts will form slowly, and they will come out extra fast or not at all. When speaking, the person may jump from one topic to the next.

Perceptual changes turn the schizophrenic's world upside down because sensory messages often become confused. These hallucinations result when the person who is ill sees, hears, smells, or tastes things that are not there. Sometimes the person will hear voices telling him or her to do things. There is always a danger that such commands will be obeyed.

When one or all five senses are affected, people's sense of self is destroyed because they have little control over their lives. It is important to remember that people who experience these changes will often try to keep them a secret. Below is a list of behaviors that some of the family members in a support group have said they noticed about their loved ones.

Checklist of Warning Signs

⇔ Loss of touch with reality

⇔ Change in personality

⇔ Irrational statements

⇔ Depression

⇔ Unexpected hostility

⇔ Withdrawal from friends or activities

⇔ Wild reactions to criticism

- Use of words that do not exist or make sense

- Sudden excesses in behavior or reaction, such as extreme anger or fear

- Dropping out of activities or out of life in general

- Extreme preoccupation with religion or the occult

- Attempts to escape life through frequent moves

- Substance abuse

- Insomnia

These signs do not necessarily mean that a person is suffering from a mental illness. Instead, they should be used as guidelines to urge families to seek advice if several of these behaviors appear in a family member.

You should keep in mind that few people with the symptoms of schizophrenia receive sympathy and understanding. Generally, early symptoms are frustrating, sometimes even repulsive, because they can be so extreme. The people around the schizophrenic person, whether it be friends or family, might think the person is acting out or just trying to get attention. The sufferer may be punished when, in fact, he or she is actually very ill and needs immediate treatment.

How Do Scientists Describe the Symptoms?

Let's look at some of the ways medical science describes the symptoms, so you will be able to communicate with doctors and understand what they are telling you.

Positive Symptoms

Angela was a thirty-year-old middle school teacher who had been hearing "God" speak to her for several years. At first, God talked to her and she talked back to him. She found the relationship very pleasing because she felt she was receiving special attention given to no one else. However, as time went on, the voice became louder and criticized her appearance. God told her to harm herself. She would bang her head against the walls at home until God told her she could stop.

One day, Angela's husband found her in the middle of one of her episodes. He thought she was having a nervous breakdown from the stress of her teaching job and took her to a psychiatrist. She was eventually diagnosed with schizophrenia.

Doctors, psychiatrists, psychotherapists, and psychologists describe behavior as positive, negative, and disorganized. In this case, the term "positive" does not mean something good, which may make it seem like a contradiction. When referring to behavior, positive means psychotic symptoms that are present but should be absent. Angela was experiencing positive or overt symptoms that could be seen by her husband. Other researchers use the term Type I for positive symptoms and Type II for negative symptoms.

Positive symptoms are most often related to schizophrenia. They are called positive because the condition has produced an abnormal event in the person's life. Such an event may include the creation of a sensation that is not actually in the environment or certain thought patterns that cannot be controlled.

Negative Symptoms

Other types of symptoms are described as negative. This means that the person lacks certain characteristics that are normally present. A negative symptom would be showing no emotion. The person may have a blank, zombielike expression or no expression at all. He or she may not be able to start or complete an activity, and his or her speech may be brief and barely coherent. Dr. Nancy Andreasen identifies five groups of negative symptoms:

- **Affective flattening or emotional blunting.** This symptom is when the individual does not express emotion, verbal or nonverbal. People normally show emotions with body language and words. The person with schizophrenia does not do this.

- **Alogia.** This negative symptom means that the person has special speech characteristics. The person says very little and rarely starts a conversation. If individuals with this symptom do produce speech, it is not meaningful, and they may have to continually restart what they are saying.

- **Avolition.** Avolition means that the person shows a lack of volition, which is the will to act at all.

- **Anhedonia.** This is the inability to have pleasure, usually also considered an antisocial characteristic.

- **Catatonia.** Catatonia is the most extreme negative symptom—an individual acts as if he or she is in a trance, and will almost appear to be in a stupor.

Delusions

A delusion is a false belief, for instance, that other people are plotting against you or threatening you in some way. Persons with delusions may think that others are reading their minds or secretly monitoring them. Sometimes, a deluded person believes that it is possible to control other people's thoughts.

James's family had recently moved into a new apartment. It was the nicest one they had ever had. However, only a few weeks after they moved in, James became convinced his thoughts were being broadcast to all of the other residents by a network of computer chips in the wall. He believed the high-tech equipment was controlled in the building's electrical generator. He made several attempts to get into the room where all the equipment was kept, but he was chased away by the night watchman. One night, after prying open the room with a crowbar, he was arrested. At the police station, James told his parents why he had broken into the room. A psychiatrist was called immediately.

Delusions can be very powerful and incredibly intricate. In James's case, his paranoia was related to technology. Sometimes people may think they are someone famous, like Napoleon or the queen of England. Other people may believe they are fictitious characters, as in our earlier example, where Lisa's brother Jason thought he was King Lear.

A schizophrenic's delusions may appear so outlandish that it seems obvious that they are not true. However, delusions are real to those who experience them. Persuading a schizophrenic that his or her delusions are not true is extremely difficult. Delusions are resistant to reason.

Disorganized Symptoms

Other symptoms are disorganized thinking patterns, mostly reflected in speech and behavior. The person's speech does not make sense or is incoherent. Movement may be very slow, or patterns like walking or pacing may be constantly repeated. Everyday sounds and sights may not make sense. Sometimes, words and moods are not in tune with each other. Speech disorganization waves a red flag to the psychiatrist that a problem is present.

"Altered sense of self" describes a person who has the sensation of being without a body. He or she may think he or she does not exist as a person or no longer recognize where the body stops and the rest of the world begins.

Vincent van Gogh was a remarkable Dutch painter who was also known to suffer from mental illness. While in a psychotic state in 1889, he painted *Starry Night.* This painting shows the distortion of color, light, and texture that some people with schizophrenia may experience.

Dealing with Symptoms

Dealing with symptoms in a loved one taxes every emotion of a family member. This is why understanding the disease is so important. Remember that your loved one may not fit into all or any of these categories.

A prognosis predicts the course and end of the disease. It may involve statistics to estimate the chance of recovery. For example, the doctor may tell you that the disease will be unrelenting and that it will progress onward from the first episode. Another prognosis could be that your loved one's schizophrenia will follow a course of psychotic flare-ups followed by remission—a time in which the person will not have any symptoms of the illness. Women tend to have the

Vincent van Gogh's *Starry Night*

latter form of the disease, with a better chance of recovery. Regardless of gender, after five to ten years, the disease usually tends to stabilize.

Finding the Right Doctor

As we discussed, family members are usually the first to notice changes in behavior. If the person shows some of the symptoms we have discussed, you should encourage your family to take action. Take the person to see your family physician as soon as possible. The person may resist the treatment because he or she will most likely insist the delusions and fantasies are real.

You should also begin to look for a doctor who is trained to treat schizophrenia. If you know about the disease and ask questions, you can find out whether you are comfortable dealing with a particular physician. If a physician thinks the behavior is "all in the head" or that the person is "trying to get attention," and lightly dismisses the behavior, you will not want to deal with this particular doctor. If a physician has little time to discuss the patient and immediately prescribes medication, most likely you will not choose to deal with this doctor either.

Your main goal is to find a doctor you feel comfortable with and believe will help your suffering family member. If you are not happy with or lack confidence in the doctor, do not hesitate to change physicians or seek a second opinion.

Although schizophrenia seems like a terrifying disease, it is important that you know its symptoms. Knowledge will give you the power to discuss the possibility of your loved one's recovery. You will be able to understand what the individual is going through and be able to discuss possible treatments with the doctor.

Effective
Communication

Schizophrenia is a condition in which the ill person thinks he or she is healthy and fine, so most of the time it is the family that must take the initiative in getting help. The family will also have to supply a lot of the information to the doctor about symptoms, changes in behavior, and hallucinations, because the ill person will most likely not be cooperative or share much information. Early intervention is extremely important.

When Jack was seventeen, his mother brought him to the family doctor. He was in good physical health, but it was clear that his mother had initiated the visit. She requested a brief word outside with the doctor. She told the doctor about how Jack had lost interest in his friends, and sports, and avoided the family whenever he could.

She also told the doctor how when she asked if there was anything wrong, he gave strange answers like "Ask me again at 2:27 AM"—or he might not answer at all. When his father heard him talking to himself in the bedroom, he insisted they make a doctor's appointment.

Jack's family made the right choice in deciding to take him to the doctor. But there were some other things they could have done to make the visit more productive. If you and your family are just beginning to deal with a schizophrenic family member, here are some tips to make your visits to your doctor more successful.

Letter to the Doctor

After an appointment is made, it is a good idea for the family to write a letter to the doctor so he or she will have some background information. The following is an example of a letter that Jack's parents could have written, giving helpful insight to the health care professional.

Dear Doctor,

On January 3, 2001, we have an appointment with you to see our son, Jack Collins. Several months ago he began to behave in an unusual manner. For example, he dropped out of the band, an activity he loved dearly. His dad heard him in a strange, intense conversation with himself. He does not sleep well at night and therefore has no energy during the day. His appearance has changed drastically, from clean to very tousled and dirty, and he has failed all of his classes this year.

I am enclosing a list of comments from his friends and some from his teachers at school.

We think medical help is necessary and are eager to talk with you.

Writing a letter is better than just showing up at the doctor's office and being unorganized in your presentation of symptoms. This way the doctor will know specifics about your family member's condition, and not just from you, but from friends and teachers as well. Look at how the above letter included specific situations that had been noticed. These specifics will help the doctor understand your family member's case better.

Diary of Treatment

When the process of treatments has begun, it is very important that the family keep a record. It can be a diary or just a record of daily happenings, also known as an anecdotal record.

Essentials of a Good Diary

- Date and time of day.

- Clear, concise description of behavior, including how long the behavior lasted, what provoked it, and how it was resolved.

- Note and date all doctor appointments and what happened at each one.

- Keep all correspondence.

The record is very important when you consult your doctor or if you change doctors. Also, keep the record confidential. If the schizophrenic has paranoid tendencies, knowing of the record may convince the person you are part of a plot. Some families may find that the person would like to write down his or her own thoughts or feelings. You can record these in the record, too.

Working with Health Professionals

The family needs to talk to the doctor. Remember, the loved one may not want to communicate, so the information given by the family will be extremely important to the evaluation. You should also rehearse your visit. Try to have everything written down. Make a list of questions that you will go through with the physician, and do not be nervous or intimidated by the doctor. The doctor is a professional and is there to help your family cope with having a schizophrenic member.

Communication

Because of the nature of schizophrenia, communication can be an intricate goal to achieve. Many families get into arguments because some members may not understand the effects of schizophrenia, and feelings are often hurt. Even families who are not dealing with psychiatric disorders have communication problems, but when coping with mental illness, tensions in the home escalate. In fact, the symptoms of the illness itself may evoke problems. Not concentrating, not listening, excessive stimuli, and delusions will interfere with communication because they cause the schizophrenic to react in strange and extreme ways. Becoming a good communicator is the best way to resolve many of the issues that a family will confront.

Learning How to Communicate

You may not think it is important to learn to communicate well, but communication is sometimes very difficult, even in everyday life. When dealing with a schizophrenic, communication is even harder. Saying things like "You've been really weird lately" or "You are really sick" does not help anyone. Suggesting that the schizophrenic person is "crazy" will only alienate him or her even more.

Neither should you suggest that family and friends have been discussing the person behind his or her back. Statements like "You are really upsetting us" or "You are making Dad really mad" blame the schizophrenic person for his or her illness. Again, this makes positive steps toward recovery more difficult.

People with good communication skills use "I" statements rather than "you" statements. They also try to focus on a particular problem that is more acceptable, like an ill person's lack of energy or his or her sadness. Say something such as "I know you haven't been sleeping well at night and are just worn out during the day. Let's make an appointment to see the doctor." This way the doctor will not be perceived as an enemy, but as someone who can help. Below you will find elements of effective communication that will help you talk with the ill person, doctor, and family members in a more constructive manner.

- Look at the person and lean in his or her direction. Have a personable expression when you speak.

- Speak warmly and accentuate positive feelings. However, do not talk down to him or her.

- Be very specific in how you want to help the person. For example: "It is very important to me that you see the doctor." Let the person know how good you would feel if he or she would do this.

- Get to the point; be clear about your concerns. Use simple, direct language.

The Shocking Crisis

The first crisis or psychotic episode is always a shock. It is terrifying to hear a relative talking about skeletons coming in the window or voices commanding him or her to take over the world. But the fact is that he or she is probably even more terrified than you are. The first episode usually occurs with little warning and a second episode will probably follow. Seek medical help as quickly as possible because the person may need to be hospitalized for a few days.

Be Prepared for the Worst

Although rare, a person with schizophrenia may get violent during an episode, and you may have to call the police. Sometimes, simply making the statement "I am calling the police" calms the person because he or she realizes things are out of control. Other times, though, you will be left without any option but to call the police.

When you phone the police, it is a good idea to tell them your loved one is in great need of help. Explain what he or she is doing—throwing chairs or making violent threats, for instance—but also tell them what you need them to do to help. Most often, the best thing you can say is that you need help getting the person to the hospital. Make sure the police are informed if your relative is armed or if there are weapons in the house. However, the most important thing you can do is stay calm and reflect how calm you are in the way you speak to the emergency operator. This way the police will know that the situation is an emergency but not completely out of control.

When the police arrive, be prepared for a variety of responses. Some officers may be trained people who have worked with psychiatric cases before, while others may have little experience in handling such a situation. Some may be very competent and sympathetic, others may appear gruff and uncaring.

Positive Actions Versus Negative Actions

Positive Actions

- Try to remain as calm as possible.

- Turn off any loud distractions such as the radio or television.

- If other people are around, quietly ask them to leave the room.

- Speak in a calm, clear voice.

- Allow the person space to move around so he or she feels free, not caged or guarded.

- Give the person choices, even if they are small ones; it will help the individual to feel in control.

Negative Actions

- Shouting at the person to calm down.

- Trying to reason with the person. Reasoning during an episode is useless.

- Looking at the individual straight in the eye. Avoid continuous eye contact because the person may interpret this as being aggressive.

- Don't block the doorway or other exit to a room. This may invite violence.

One thing you must do is record everything that happens—how long it took for them to respond; the officers' names and badge numbers; and how they handled the situation. You should also contact the doctor and let him or her know about the episode. The doctor may want to meet with the person at the hospital. Be sure that you inform the doctor that you will be at the hospital, too.

As frightening as it may sound, now is the time for you to plan for an emergency. You should also be practicing how to talk with medical professionals and the person with schizophrenia. All of these skills will help you greatly when you are dealing with an episode.

Diagnosis

Dear Dr. Martinez,

Thank you for responding to my first letter about Jason. We took your advice and brought him home from college to keep an eye on him. Just like you said he would, Jason had an episode.

Earlier this afternoon we were eating lunch, and Jason started screaming that he saw snakes coming in the window and started hitting the floor with a chair. We called the police. I cried when I saw him arrested like a common criminal.

I am writing this as we sit in the waiting room of the hospital. I still don't believe he has schizophrenia. Why is this happening to us? We are a good family.

Lisa

After reading Lisa's letter to Dr. Martinez, it is apparent that the family is trying to deny that Jason has schizophrenia. This is the first hurdle they must jump—acceptance of the situation. Many families have a difficult time accepting that their loved one has schizophrenia. Some are scared that the behavior will embarrass the family. These feelings must be dealt with, but first you must concentrate on getting your loved one properly diagnosed.

What Does a Good Diagnosis Include?

Making a diagnosis is not as easy as it sounds. If the person has had an episode like Jason's, you may think he would be diagnosed with schizophrenia immediately, but this is not how it usually happens. Diagnosing schizophrenia is a long process. It may be evident simply by talking that the person has auditory or visual hallucinations, but for a well-documented diagnosis, several things should be included.

History and Mental Status

An evaluation of the person's history and mental status is one of the first steps in making a diagnosis. This is done routinely during admission to the hospital, but it needs to be thorough and complete. Most times, family members can provide essential information. The following are some typical questions that are asked:

- ⇔ Have there been any head injuries?

- ⇔ Have headaches occurred often?

- ⇔ How is the person's general body health?

- ⇔ What drugs, if any, is he or she using?

Neurological Exams

A neurological exam should also be given. For example, a series of tests may be given where the person is asked to write or draw. This may screen out conditions such as brain tumors or Huntington's disease—a severe neurological condition that usually appears around the age of thirty.

Laboratory Tests

Laboratory tests should also be part of the diagnosis. Tests that might be run include a complete blood count (CBC), which may reveal conditions such as anemia, AIDS, or exposure to lead or other harmful chemicals. A urinalysis can reveal the use of street and other drugs.

Psychological Tests and Physiological Tests

While some acutely ill patients may not be able to take psychological tests because they are too ill for this type of evaluation, psychological testing may be useful in determining borderline cases. Brain scans or, more specifically, MRI or PET scans may be used to determine exactly what illness the person is suffering from. Some rare diseases as well as brain tumors may be located with these scans.

Another form of brain test that may be used is called an electroencephalogram, or EEG. Electrodes are placed on the head, and brain waves are measured. These brain wave tests are used along with cerebrospinal fluid studies, also called lumbar punctures, in which a needle is used to draw spinal fluid for study. These tests are useful in ruling out viral diseases such as multiple sclerosis (MS).

Technology in this area is improving very rapidly and is becoming more efficient and sophisticated with each passing day. This means that in the coming years even better tests are going to be available.

Meet the DSM-IV

The definition of schizophrenia is explained in a manual called the *Diagnostic and Statistical Manual of Mental Disorders (DSM-IV)*. It was written by a task force of the American Psychiatric Association and has been revised many times. The "IV" means it is the fourth revision. The guidelines are very specific; if the noted criteria are not met, a diagnosis may not be given. Your doctor may refer you to the *DSM-IV* so that you can read about the symptoms of schizophrenia and other mental disorders. Within the *DSM-IV*, there are six major criteria that define schizophrenia, called diagnostic criteria.

What Are Characteristic Symptoms?
These symptoms are massive disruptions in thought, perception, emotion, and motor behavior. The disruptions may be bizarre beliefs, delusions, or hallucinations. Some kinds of hallucinations may not be obvious. To fit the description of characteristic symptoms, hallucinations must occur in the presence of others or with marked disturbances of speech, motor activity, or emotional response.

What Are Some Other Diagnostic Criteria?
A person must reflect the symptoms over a period of time. The person also must show decreased ability to function at work and in social relations, and growing difficulty in taking care of himself or herself. Basically, schizophrenia cannot be diagnosed if the symptoms do not interfere with daily life, and continuous signs of the illness must occur for at least six months. The physician may bring the person back for many anecdotal observations. During this six-month period, the person is said to have a "schizophreniform disorder." Only after a person exhibits two characteristic symptoms and fulfills all the other diagnostic criteria can a physician say that the condition has been differentiated, or diagnosed.

What Are Exclusion Factors?

If any one of the conditions that mimic schizophrenia is present, a diagnosis cannot be made. Such conditions are called exclusion factors because they affirm that the person does not have schizophrenia; instead, the individual has a different problem.

As we discussed, drug abuse is one of the factors that may cause symptoms that mirror schizophrenia. In particular, there are some drugs called psychotomimetic, which means they cause symptoms that are very similar to the symptoms of schizophrenia. The effects of these drugs were first described in 1919, but most of the research was done in the early 1960s. Psychedelic drugs such as synthetic LSD and natural hallucinogens such as peyote and mescaline can also mimic symptoms of schizophrenia. The superamphetamines found within the drugs produce the same effects. LSD, for example, may cause the individual to see or hear things that are not there.

Epilepsy is a condition in which the brain waves become frenzied and sporadic, causing seizures to occur. A person with epilepsy often becomes very depressed, and during a seizure the effects resemble schizophrenia.

Brain tumors are growths in any area of the brain that can cause changes in behavior and personality. Wilson's disease is a hereditary disease that causes an individual's mental capacity to deteriorate.

There are also many other mental illnesses that must be ruled out. Bipolar depression, sometimes known as manic-depressive illness, is characterized by wide mood swings. At one moment the person may be excited, upbeat, and enthusiastic and a moment later be sad, depressed, and uncaring. Patients with schizoaffective disorder have symptoms of both bipolar disorder and schizophrenia.

It cannot be overemphasized that the diagnosis may not come immediately. It will probably take a long time, because ruling out all exclusion factors can be a very complex process. Symptoms necessary for diagnosis may not be recognized on the first visit. Some symptoms may not show up until the condition is advanced. In addition, an individual's personality plays an integral role in the evaluation.

Support Groups

As you can see, schizophrenia is a variable illness, meaning it can take on many forms with many different symptoms. While you are waiting for a diagnosis, support groups may be one of the best sources of information and encouragement. These are groups of people who have banded together and meet regularly to discuss symptoms, treatment, and coping skills.

A good resource in the United States is the National Alliance for the Mentally Ill (NAMI). Ask the members in your area to relate their experiences with local physicians and psychiatrists. They can be the best sources for recommending a good psychiatrist. You can find the address and Web site of this support group and many other helpful organizations in the Where to Go for Help section at the end of this book.

Finding Your Health Team

Generally, your first contact will be with a family doctor or general practitioner (GP). Many GPs do not have a lot of experience with mental illness, so they will recommend that you find a psychiatrist or psychologist to treat your family member.

In order for you to find a good doctor as quickly as possible, start by talking with people who have dealt with a schizophrenic family member and have gone through the process you are just beginning. A good place to begin is with a local support group. You can find local support groups in the telephone book under Mental Health, or you can call the health department.

When you contact a doctor, ask the following questions:

⤳ Do you believe schizophrenia is a brain disease?

⤳ How do you screen for other possible illnesses?

⤳ What tests will you give?

⤳ What antipsychotic medicines do you use?

⤳ What has been your experience with the newer medicines?

⤳ Are you interested in the patient's entire welfare and do you know about referrals for alternative methods of care?

⤳ How will you involve the family in the treatment process?

⤳ What do you think causes schizophrenia?

⤳ How important do you think psychotherapy is in treating schizophrenia?

⤳ What are your feelings on rehabilitation?

When you are speaking with the doctor, if you do not get the answers you want or do not feel comfortable with the doctor, you should try someone else. While you do want someone who is medically competent, you must also find someone who has empathy and an understanding of the condition. Finally, you want a doctor who will work well with your mentally ill family member and with you.

Who's Who on Your Health Team

Psychiatrists
The psychiatrist is generally the person who directs the treatment. A psychiatrist is a doctor of medicine (MD) who spends years in residency and has special training in psychiatry. Only MDs can prescribe medication. Not all psychiatrists work with people with serious psychosis.

Psychologists
Psychologists have six or eight years of postgraduate training and have a Ph.D., or doctorate, in psychology. While they do not prescribe medicine, they consult and counsel during the process of rehabilitation.

Psychiatric Nurses
Psychiatric nurses are registered nurses (RNs) who specialize in working with psychiatric patients. RNs are usually employed at hospitals that specialize in mental illness or are in charge of the floors in hospitals that are devoted to mental health.

Psychiatric Social Workers
People trained in social services work with the rest of the team in providing social support and individual care. Most have a postgraduate degree in social work.

Prognosis

After you have received the diagnosis, you will be interested in what will happen in the future. Prognosis is a subject that should be discussed with the doctor, so that you have an idea of what to expect. Questions about the prognosis might include the following: what are the chances of recovery, how independent is the person likely to be, and how can we as a family prepare for the future. Although there is no way to predict the future, the doctor can look at some predictors.

Personality before illness. If the person was always a loner, most likely he or she will not turn into a social butterfly.

Gender. Women tend to respond to treatment better than men.

Family history. If there is no history of schizophrenia in the family, the chance for recovery is increased.

Age of onset. The younger the age, the less chance for recovery.

Timing. The best outcomes are those in which the onset was sudden.

Symptoms. Some are more suggestive of a good outcome than others.

Early treatment. One positive indicator is early recognition, diagnosis, and, therefore, early treatment.

Living with Schizophrenia

I felt very alone, alone with my craziness. I had suffered for over twenty-five years with hallucinations, delusions, and paranoia. In fact, there has never been a time before now that I can remember when my life was my own.

I had one particular friend from the time I was twelve years old. He was my secret pal. I felt really special having his attention. I could hear him and talk to him when no one else would listen.

When I went away to college, my friend began to demand all of my time and energy. He would yell at me when I did something he didn't like and made me feel terrible. I couldn't stop his screaming. The voice inside my head was so loud at times I couldn't hear what anyone else was saying. So I tried to hide it. What would people think of me if they found out? To this day, I still don't know how I made it through college.

JoAnn is a thirty-year-old woman who lives in Chicago and is now on medication. She has a full-time job as a writer and editor. JoAnn has pointed out some of the problems a person with schizophrenia faces: the secret friend, the relationship that develops, and how often and loud the voices can be.

What Is It Like to Have Schizophrenia?

The experiences of people with schizophrenia are varied. However, when they talk about the illness, their feelings are not like what many intelligent people imagine they would be. For instance, in 1681, the poet John Dryden wrote in the *Spanish Friar*, "there is a pleasure sure in being mad which none but the madmen know." One thing that all people with schizophrenia would agree on is that many people do not understand the pain and problems of living in a fantasy world.

Frederick J. Frese is a clinical psychologist who also has schizophrenia. Diagnosed at the age of twenty-two, he lectures and encourages those with mental illness. He tells how a person with schizophrenia can deal with the obstacles he or she will undoubtedly face.

When Dr. Frese speaks, he always relates that he was hospitalized five times before he was willing to consider even the slightest possibility that anything was wrong with him.

One of the most difficult things for a person to accept is that he or she has a mental disorder. It is also the nature of the disorder that unbalanced chemistry controls thought and action. When examining schizophrenia from a sympathetic perspective, one can see how difficult it would be to admit that your mind is playing tricks on you. That is why convincing a mentally ill person to accept the problem is very difficult. Yet acceptance is one of the first things people must do to recover. Once they have accepted that they are ill, they will be able to start learning about their disorder.

Sense and Sensibility

Some people with schizophrenia say that their sensations are altered.

- Colors are brighter, almost fluorescent.

- Everything looks vibrantly red.

- Faces take on a hideous appearance, like people having fangs.

- When people speak, the mind is overloaded.

- Increased sense of touch, feelings of electricity.

Terror

Some people describe schizophrenia as a terrifying journey through a world of madness that no one can understand. The journey is empty and deranged. There are no anchors to reality.

Studies have shown that when given psychological tests, schizophrenics have poor attention spans and difficulty concentrating on one task at a time. They also have problems forming concepts, thinking abstractly, and remembering things. Can you imagine doing mental tasks with a voice like JoAnn described screaming inside of your head?

Margaret received a degree in education and was teaching third grade when the voices started. They sounded like computers or the voices of robots. They were funny at first because they sounded so strange. She liked the voices and soon became engrossed in her fantasy world. She had to leave her job and ended up in a psychiatric hospital for four months. She spent most of her time engrossed in the world of the voices.

In the hospital, Margaret did not trust anyone, especially her first female therapist. The doctor encouraged her to open up, but she did not want to be labeled crazy. Even though she trusted no one, she felt blessed when she was talking and listening to the voices.

What Are Delusions and Hallucinations Like?

Schizophrenic delusions are false ideas believed by a patient but not accepted by anyone else. For example, a schizophrenic might think that every time another person scratches his or her nose, a personal message is being sent, or every time someone coughs, a person is communicating with aliens.

Although most everyone experiences paranoid thinking at one time or another, delusions without any basis or reason, in which a person believes he or she is being watched, persecuted, or attacked, are called paranoid delusions. Delusions and hallucinations are usually in the context of the culture in which a person lives.

Changes in Emotion

People with schizophrenia who appear to have no emotions may be experiencing turmoil and pain that we cannot interpret. One study indicated that schizophrenics process emotions differently than people who do not suffer from the illness. When shown photographs of different emotions, it was very hard for schizophrenics to verbally describe the emotion. These problems may be linked to the difficulty many schizophrenics have in forming social relationships.

Stress and Excitement

People recovering or responding to treatment often describe how they are overstimulated when confronted with exciting circumstances. Some schizophrenics say that visits to the mall cause stress because there is a lot of external stimulation. Holidays or family gatherings also tend to generate too much excitement. If a schizophrenic knows he or she is going to be in a stressful situation, it may be helpful to ask the doctor for suggestions on how to deal with the environment effectively.

Hobbies

Many people with schizophrenia find it helpful to engage in creative activities that do not necessarily require logical thinking. Music, art, and poetry are fulfilling activities. In fact, artist Mike Jaffe designed a series of posters highlighting people with mental illness who led very enriched lives. Composer Robert Schumann, dancer Vaslav Nijinski, and playwright Eugene O'Neill are some of the talented people who are included.

How Would You Deal with the Stigma of Mental Illness?

It is harder to share with people that you have a mental illness than it is to tell of an illness like cancer or heart disease. Most people, because of the stigma that still surrounds mental illness, would be sympathetic and understanding about cancer and be uncomfortable about mental illness. They might treat you like you are crazy, or they might be frightened of your behavior.

The National Mental Health Consumers' Association recently adopted a national agenda. The top goal on the organization's list is to decrease "discrimination, abuse, ostracism, stigmatization and other forms of social prejudice" that affect people with mental illness.

The Right to Public Education

If a person with a disorder is still in high school or grades K–12, he or she falls under the Americans with Disabilities Act (ADA) of 1990 and the Individuals with Disabilities Education Act (IDEA) of 1997. These acts ensure that school districts place students with disabilities in the least restricted environment in the school, which could be regular classes or special education classes.

These laws are written and enforced by the federal government, and they are personalized to comply with the needs for educating a student with a disability. Schizophrenia is specifically named within the text.

Employment Problems

In general, the world of work places many demands on people. Adjusting to supervisors, handling customers, being on time, and taking orders are all part of being employed, but they cause stress, too. The schizophrenic person also has to deal with any prejudice that arises at work. Although most people will understand and accept the schizophrenic, evaluating the person by performance and not illness, there might be people who are prejudiced.

After five years in and out of treatment in a psychiatric hospital, Mark was stabilized and earned a bachelor's degree in accounting at the community college. After graduation when Mark started looking for a job, he was never offered a position. Whenever he explained the many years during which he had not held a job, the employer lost interest in his application.

Six months after he started searching, Mark was finally hired by a mental health services provider and has been a successful accountant for them for over two years.

Most of the employers who did not offer Mark a job were most likely looking at his condition and not his capabilities. Most schizophrenics surmise that the stigma of mental illness is almost as bad as having to deal with the disease. Only recently, the Americans with Disabilities Act (ADA) has increased employment opportunities for the mentally ill.

Social Security and Welfare

In the United States and other countries, people with schizophrenia who cannot work may qualify for certain benefits if they apply. A person who is applying for assistance—which is your legal right—should take along a friend or family member to interviews. The application process is long and frustrating, so in order to sustain motivation, it is always helpful to bring someone who will offer support and insight.

Homelessness

Anna went to a community support group every week. She never spoke. But one night, she broke down and told her story: Her daughter had schizophrenia and one day she had just disappeared.

"I felt so guilty for feeling a sense of relief, but it was. What a relief not to have someone telling me she hates me and wants to kill me. What a relief to know my own daughter won't be accusing me of plotting against her.

"Six months ago, I got a call from the police in Las Vegas. They had found my daughter asleep in an alley and she was freezing to death. She had been homeless every single day, every single night. In the hospital, they had found a slip of paper with a telephone number on it. It was mine.

"When they called, my heart soared. I had spent so many nights hoping Eliza was OK. Since she has been home, she goes to therapy every other day and is on medication. So far, she has had only two episodes."

Juveniles who run away from home usually leave after family arguments or because they simply don't want to follow the rules. Some people with schizophrenia may feel closed in or trapped, so they run away from home, wrongly thinking they will escape their loneliness.

E. Fuller Torrey is one of the world's most respected writers about schizophrenia. In his book *Nowhere to Go: The Tragic Odyssey of the Homeless Mentally Ill,* he talks about how the mentally ill are heavily represented among the homeless. SANE, a support group located in both Britain and Australia, estimates that 40 percent of the homeless have mental illness and at least one-third of these people have schizophrenia.

In the 1960s, Thorazine and other antipsychotic drugs restored some hope of recovery to mentally ill patients living in state hospitals. However, when hospital funding was cut, about 433,000 patients nationwide were released to communities that were not prepared to handle them. Although the communities were supposed to check up on and keep in contact with these people, most did not. A complete explanation of why this happened can be found in chapter 7, which discusses deinstitutionalization.

Once a person is homeless, his or her life becomes a spiral that plummets further and further downward. Without an address or money, the person can get little or no medical attention and job hunting is impossible. In order to escape the reality of their lives, most homeless people resort to drugs and alcohol. Even if the schizophrenic person never drank excessively or experimented with drugs before, being homeless is a horrible existence and often creates alcoholics and drug users.

Don't Judge Me: I Am Not My Diagnosis

Early on, many schizophrenics struggle with their sickness. They think all they are is a schizophrenic and that they no longer have a self or a personality. They think they are their diagnosis.

As time passes, they realize that schizophrenia is a part of them, but not all of them. They realize that they still have character, intelligence, and humor. Within them are all of the qualities that were there before they were diagnosed. They are still a dog lover, a dedicated friend, or an excellent reader.

People with schizophrenia are not only their illness. Just like anyone else who has a disease, he or she is still the same person as before. Friends and family should strive to remember this and work to promote this type of thinking throughout their community.

Treatment

At age eight, Brandon was diagnosed as schizo-phrenic. He had been a loner from infancy and would sometimes cry for hours for no reason. He believed that classmates could see through his clothes and that people on the covers of magazines were staring at him. At age thirteen, he believed that the old Russian leaders Czar Nicholas II, Lenin, and Trotsky were reading his mind. Even though treatment after treat-ment was tried, none helped to diminish his severe symptoms. In the early 1990s when clozapine was introduced, Brandon was put on it and the results were close to full recovery. Brandon now speaks to groups, encouraging them to continue the fight for more mental illness research.

A person can lead a fulfilling life even if he or she suf-fers from schizophrenia. As Brandon's story illustrates, although schizophrenia is not yet a curable disease, it is treatable. Clozapine is one of the first major innovations in medications for schizophrenia. Although people who take it must pay close attention to their white blood cell count, most are able to function without delusions and hallucina-tions. Since the disease is variable, many different treat-ments are in existence that treat the numerous symptoms of schizophrenia.

The World of Medications

The role of medication is to stabilize the disease. Many people have difficulty finding the right medication because some medications have unpleasant side effects. Most people find the medication that works best for them by a trial and error search.

Trying to understand the many medications that are out there is extremely confusing to a person who does not work in the field. It can be very helpful to be familiar with some of the terms that mental health professionals use. Mental health professionals refer to medications for treating the psychotic symptoms of schizophrenia as antipsychotics. "Anti" means against, and "psychotic" is the abnormal behavior. Occasionally, these medications will be referred to as neuroleptics.

Standard Antipsychotics

These medications have been around for a number of years and were first introduced in the 1950s. They may be helpful for certain symptoms, but they do not elevate motivation or emotional expressiveness. Haloperidol (Haldol), chlorpromazine (Thorazine), Mellaril, Modecate, Prolixin, Navane, and Stelazine are all examples of antipsychotics that are used to treat schizophrenia. Brand names will usually have a capital letter with a symbol to indicate it is the registered trademark of a company.

Side Effects

Like all medications, an antipsychotic may have unwanted side effects along with great benefits. During the early phases of intake, a person may experience drowsiness, restlessness, muscle spasms, tremors, dry mouth, or blurred

Why People Resist Taking Medication

⇔ They may be denying they are ill.

⇔ The medicine makes them sick or upset.

⇔ They may feel the medication is an outside force that will control them. When they are on medication, they see reality, but they may feel more comfortable in their dream world.

⇔ Medication may reduce their energy.

vision. It is also common to become depressed and for symptoms to appear worse in the beginning. Lowering the dosage can alleviate most side effects, but if depression persists, the person may have to go on an antidepressant medication like Prozac or Paxil.

Long-term side effects are neurological side effects called extrapyramidal symptoms (EPS). They may be akinesia or slowed movement, akathesia or restless limbs, or tardive dyskinesia (TD), a disorder characterized by involuntary movements of the body. About 15 to 20 percent of people on older antipsychotics may experience these side effects. More recent antipsychotics do not cause as many long-term side effects.

Atypical Antipsychotics

Since 1990, a number of new antipsychotic drugs have been introduced. They are called atypical antipsychotics. The term "atypical" means they are different from the older antipsychotics. They have a different chemical makeup, work in different ways, and help stabilize the symptoms more quickly.

Risperidone (Risperdal) is generally considered as first-line treatment for a newly diagnosed patient. It is considered a safer drug because it has fewer side effects, but it is not as effective as clozapine. Fifteen years ago, this was the first drug to be approved by the Federal Drug Administration (FDA) to treat schizophrenia.

In comparison, clozapine (Clozaril) is very effective, but has a possibility of severe side effects. The primary one is a loss of white blood cells, the cells that your body uses to fight infection. The patient must be monitored with blood tests every one to two weeks.

Finally, olanzapine (Zyprexa) is a recently approved medication with encouraging reports. The drug has a high rate of efficacy, or effectiveness, and a low side effect profile. There are now thirty atypical antipsychotics being researched, so there will be many more in the near future.

How Long Should People Take Antipsychotic Drugs?

Families sometimes worry about their loved ones taking medications because they think they will become addicted. The fact is that these medications are not there to promote mind control or act like a "chemical straightjacket." All antipsychotic medication does is block the neurotransmitter receptors, which diminishes hallucinations, agitation, confusion, and delusions.

Drugs also reduce the risk of future psychotic episodes, or relapses in schizophrenics who have recovered from an acute episode. Even with medication, some may still have a relapse. Even higher relapse rates are recorded when medication is suddenly discontinued—instead of weaning

Dr. Clozapine

In 1975, Dr. Herbert Y. Meltzer, while working in his laboratory, found a new substance to replace the old medication Thorazine, which he thought was inadequate. His experiment with rats showed him that the new medication might work in treating cases of mental illness. People were so impressed by his discovery that they started calling him Dr. Clozapine.

The drug was scheduled for massive tests, but in the summer of 1975, hospitals in Finland began to report deaths among those taking the drug. There was evidence of agranulocytosis, a component that affects the white blood cells. The trials were canceled and it was back to the drawing board. The FDA finally approved clozapine in the early 1990s.

the person from it—and when drugs are taken irregularly. The person must adhere to the treatment plan because the consequences can be very damaging.

Nonbiological Therapies

Not all psychiatrists and doctors agree on therapies. Some are completely committed to psychotherapy without the use of drugs, whereas others believe that a good treatment program includes both. Some may ask the individual to recall events from childhood, while many others use a nondirect approach in which the therapist says little but helps the person gain insight into the past and present. Other discussions may deal with specific day-to-day problems like finding a job.

The American Psychiatric Association Commission on Psychotherapies addresses the value of psychotherapy in schizophrenia treatment. In a major study, it was concluded that psychotherapy by itself is not an effective treatment for schizophrenia. However, it is useful as an adjunct treatment.

Behavior Therapy

This therapy focuses on the person with schizophrenia dealing with social situations. People with schizophrenia have many problems in this area, and many do not seek out social interaction because of their insecurities and fears. This type of treatment must be tailored to each individual.

Reward and Punishment

This therapy takes as its model the behaviorist philosophy of B.F. Skinner, who used a system of reward and punishment on animals to modify their behavior. During this therapy, a person may receive chips or tokens for correct behavior. The difficulty with behaviorist training is that it is hard to translate into the activities of everyday life.

Social Skills Training

This training tries to teach social skills in a group setting. Generally, the therapist will teach patients how to use effective verbal and nonverbal behavior in social situations. There are also a number of tasks that involve observing, analyzing, and practicing social behavior.

Each session begins with a review of what was learned in the last session and everyone is asked to share, especially if the person was able to use the behavior outside the training setting. The issues for the day are presented using videos and role-playing. After these discussions, patients are asked to set a reasonable goal to practice in their daily life.

Family Therapy
While the family may not be the cause of schizophrenia, family members are very involved in the treatment. Positive

Treatment Reminders

⤷ **Get help as early as possible**. Large-scale studies have shown that early intervention may prevent long-term illness.

⤷ **Hospitalization.** Acute symptoms such as episodes may require more intensive treatment.

⤷ **Schizophrenics should stick with their treatment.** Eighty percent of schizophrenics who stop taking medications will have a relapse within a year.

⤷ **Increase chances for recovery.** Studies show that after ten years of treatment, one-fourth of schizophrenics who have complied with treatment have almost completely recovered.

family behavior has positive effects on the therapy of the schizophrenic. It is also a good idea if the family is included in planning the treatment program. You can help by finding all the resources that are available in your community. For example, being knowledgeable about day programs, self-help groups, recreation programs, and businesses in the community that hire and work with people who have mental illness will provide you and your family member with many advantages.

Treatment Settings

⇨ **Hospital.** May be a state institution, private institution, or county hospital; may be locked or unlocked.

⇨ **Skilled nursing facility.** These facilities offer twenty-four-hour supervision and are locked.

⇨ **Halfway house.** A residential treatment program, but can be used only for a limited time.

⇨ **Board and care.** Small, homelike environment for those who can take responsibility for their own care.

⇨ **Assisted independent living.** Requires a great deal of self-care, although counselors may be on hand to resolve conflicts.

⇨ **Home.** Don't forget that the community may also offer certain services.

Treatment is incredibly important to the life of a schizophrenic. At times, the person may become frustrated, but that is when you must be most supportive. Remind the person that treatment will improve his or her life, and guide hi or her in following the steps listed below. If implemented, these steps will reduce symptoms and improve quality of life.

- Learn the names, dosages, and proper times medications are to be taken each day.
- Place medications where they will be seen regularly.
- Remind your loved one to take his or her medication.
- See that he or she stores daily doses in a pillbox with sections for the days of the week.
- Tell the doctor when your loved one is having trouble taking the medications or is not satisfied with them. Work together to find a better treatment plan.
- Do not let him or her stop taking medications or change doses without the advice of a doctor.
- If symptoms worsen or there are side effects, call his or her doctor.
- Help him or her to concentrate on goals.

History of
Mental Illness

The study and treatment of mental illness has gone through many stages to arrive at the knowledge we currently have. The stigma of mental illness—the perception that those who are mentally ill are crazy lunatics and that they cannot function within society—has roots that are traceable through history. Many of the homeless found in major cities and now in the suburbs are mentally ill. This development also has historical roots in one of our failed social experiments.

To help you gain the best perspective and understanding, we will explore the perception of mental illness throughout history. This chapter will address some of the people and movements that contributed to current developments in the area of mental health.

Early Ideas of Madness

The idea of "madness" has roots in ancient history. Around 400 BC, the Greek physician Hippocrates proposed that the imbalance of body fluids—blood, phlegm, yellow bile, and black bile—caused illness. His hypothesis was that mental disorders were caused by an imbalance of black bile, or melan chole. From this, we get the word "melancholy," which means sad or depressed.

During the Middle Ages, people with mental illness were thought to be witches who had the stigmata diaboli, or mark of the devil. Witches were killed by burning, hanging, or drowning. Mentally ill people would also be placed in prisons or welfare institutions called poorhouses.

People with mental illness were also portrayed in various forms of art, particularly within plays and drama. Two of Shakespeare's tragic characters, King Lear and Ophelia, were essentially normal people who became "mad."

Treatment in the Community
Before the 1800s, families and communities, especially in rural areas, took care of people with mental illnesses. Treatment of mental illness was not a specialty, and general doctors would handle it as part of their regular practice. However, both in America and in Europe, deciding who was "mad" was more of a community effort than a medical one.

If a family could not cope with their mentally ill member, a caregiver or custodian would take over the duties, or sometimes they would put the "maniac" in jail. Sometimes, they would even just put the person on the road or send him or her packing into the woods or over to the next village.

In some cities, religious and charitable institutions cared for mentally ill people, although these places did not provide medical treatment.

Bedlam

Over the years, "hospitals," called madhouses or lunatic hospitals, were developed for people with mental illness. Hospitals in France like Bicetre (for men) and Saltpetriere (for women) joined London's Bethlem as places that were known for their cruelty and neglect. The local people called Bethlem "Bedlam," which came to represent a place of chaos, confusion, and torture. For the average person, treatment at Bedlam was a punishment that provoked even more mental problems. By the late 1700s, however, medical people began to question the harsh treatment that the mentally ill were receiving.

After the French Revolution, when loyalists who supported Louis XVI were rounded up and executed, a tailor became convinced he was going to be beheaded on the guillotine. He knew he was innocent, but he thought people were plotting against him. He became obsessed with his delusions. Finally, he was committed to Bicetre in Paris and was treated in the same harsh manner as all the other patients.

A new doctor named Phillipe Pinel (1745-1826) changed the course of mental illness treatments when he prescribed occupational therapy and arranged for the tailor to mend the clothes of other patients. Pinel also arranged for a mock trial at which three doctors dressed as judges and declared the tailor's patriotism impeccable. He was assured that no one was going to behead him. The mock trial and occupational therapy worked, and the tailor improved drastically.

Pinel also ordered chains to be removed from the patients and ushered in a philosophy of humane treatment. He sought to convince people that patients were "mad" only in one area, so they still retained "normal" feelings in other areas. In England, a British merchant named William Tuke expressed views similar to Pinel's when he proclaimed outrage toward the treatment of the mentally ill in Britain.

Patients and Asylums

By the early nineteenth century, patients were being integrated into communities and given jobs. Around this time, the term "moral management"—aiming to remove delusions by providing creative distractions—came to be widely accepted. However, mental illness was still considered a moral flaw. The number of patients who were institutionalized boomed in the 1800s. One American asylum had 10,000 patients, and one in London had 12,000 patients.

Theories and Beliefs

In the middle of the nineteenth century, psychiatry came into being, and French and German schools began to teach the fundamentals of this new science.

A German, Wilhelm Geisinger (1817-1868), sought to unify neurology and mental medicine into one scientific discipline. "All mental illness is rooted in brain disease," he said, and his approach became known as brain psychiatry. His idea that mental illness was a brain affliction and not an affected mind was very much ahead of its time. He remade the image of people with mental illness; he saw them as regular patients with physical disorders and worked to reverse the traditional notions of asylum care.

In the 1800s, Austrian psychiatrist Sigmund Freud introduced the idea that the unconscious mind influences behavior and personality. Freud and psychoanalysis became extremely popular, so the belief that the mentally ill have repressed feelings and memories became widely accepted.

Mental Illness and Biology

In an obscure hospital in Munich, a doctor with a handlebar mustache spent much of his time scribbling down notes on thousands of cases. Dr. Emil Kraepelin (1856-1926) tried to push psychiatry in a different direction by studying and classifying mental disorders. His influential textbooks were forerunners of the statistical and diagnostic manual discussed in chapters 1 and 4.

Kraepelin also introduced the diagnosis of dementia praecox, the first recognition of schizophrenia. The term means premature deterioration of the intellectual faculties, and although it is no longer in use, you may see it used in older textbooks. Kraepelin noted that the condition began in youth and created a dulling of the senses, withdrawal, and listlessness.

He also examined many other cases of mental illness and devised two major categories: manic-depressives, who were curable, and schizophrenics, whom he labeled with his classification of dementia praecox. Whereas his rival Sigmund Freud had proposed that these mental illnesses were emotion-based or psychosocial, Dr. Kraepelin became convinced these patients had an illness that was biological in nature. He soon became known as the father of biological psychiatry. Unfortunately, he held the destructive belief that schizophrenics were hopelessly incurable and genetically dangerous to the German state. He became an early proponent of racial purity and an advocate of eugenics, a science that deals with the improvement of hereditary qualities of a race, usually by controlling reproduction.

Kraepelin's academic research led to the work of the second great researcher of schizophrenia, Eugen Bleuler (1857-1937). A Swiss psychiatrist, he coined the term "schizophrenia" and connected it to delusions and hallucinations. The root "schizo" was meant to signify a split from reality. The term turned out to be a bit confusing, because people began to associate it with split, or multiple, personalities.

Two more recent theories have also contributed to the confusing mix of beliefs about schizophrenia. Thomas

Szasz, an American psychoanalyst, proclaimed schizophrenia to be a set of behaviors and not a disease. He also determined that all other mental illnesses were in this category. R. D. Laing, a British psychiatrist, supported the idea that a person with schizophrenia was really the one that was sane, and that schizophrenia was the way healthy people responded to an insane world. Laing also claimed that schizophrenics acted out because they were burdened with terrible stress.

Primitive Diagnoses and Treatments

When the term "stigmata" came into the psychiatric vocabulary, many nineteenth-century psychiatrists supported the idea that appearance, especially facial features, could help diagnose mental illness. A person's condition was recognized and diagnosed by external signs, or stigmata. By examining a face, the doctor would pronounce the person insane. When cameras became available, photographs of faces were taken and prepared to assist in the diagnosis.

While people with mental illnesses were no longer kept in filthy cages in asylums, some treatments in the early part of the twentieth century were still inhumane. The practice of giving purgatives, or large doses of laxatives, to "clean you out" was still in use from the days when it was believed that a person was mentally ill because poisons had built up in his or her body. It was felt that laxatives would release these toxins.

Treatments were also very strange and not yet scientifically proven. In many cases, bandages were placed around the head to heal the brain into the right activity. Another extreme solution was infecting the person with malaria, while another was giving hot and cold baths. Sedatives such as chloral

hydrate were also used. Some terrible experimental procedures such as creating insulin shock and performing a prefrontal lobotomy—an operation where the front section of the
brain is removed—were also introduced.

French anthropologist Benedict Augustin Morel (1809-1873)
spread alarm about the degeneration of the human race among
the great thinkers of the time. German, French, British, and
American intellectuals began to consider how they could protect humanity's genetic stock.

Suddenly psychiatry became society's policeman and
gatekeeper. Sir Francis Galton (1822-1911) developed the
idea of eugenics, improving society by improving heredity.
This, combined with the fanaticism of the Nazi Party in
Germany, led to one of the darkest episodes in the history
of medicine.

Involuntary Sterilization

The idea of sterilizing the mentally ill began in America
when fears of being overrun by immigrants focused on
genetics and degeneration. In 1907, the state of Indiana
passed the first legislation for sterilization of the mentally
ill and the criminally insane. Twenty-seven other states
soon followed. By 1939, over 30,000 people were steril-
ized involuntarily.

Changing Mental Health Care

The turning point of the century was World War II, which
lasted from 1941 through 1945. After the war, there was a
great upheaval in people's consciousness about civil rights
and the rights of patients in hospitals. Some people began to
question and expose mental health care standards.

On May 6, 1946, *Life* magazine published a thirteen-page exposé on state hospitals entitled "Bedlam: 1946." Pictures of filthy and rat-infested hospitals shocked the consciences of the country. Some likened the hospitals to the Nazi concentration camps. Postwar writers included Albert Q. Maisel, who wrote "Bedlam: 1946"; Mary Jane Ward, who wrote her autobiography, *In the Snake Pit;* and Albert Deutsch, who wrote *The Shame of the States.* The idea of undercover exposés, however, had originated many years earlier, in 1887, when a New York *World* writer named Nellie Bly went into a mental hospital and came out with a sensational story called "Ten Days in a Madhouse."

The antipsychotics, especially chlorpromazine and reserpine, were discovered in the 1940s. With their use in the 1950s and 1960s, people said that the mentally ill could be treated and released, and would be well in six months. Before 1960, people were treated with long-term stays in mental hospitals. The new medicines, coupled with political pressure to reduce cost, led to a concept called deinstitutionalization, which called for taking people out of hospitals and placing them in community treatment centers. Dr. E. Fuller Torrey, in his book *Surviving Schizophrenia,* reveals his opinion on deinstitutionalization, when he calls it "the great failure of the twentieth century."

The administration of President John F. Kennedy provided the funds for establishing community mental health centers and emptying the hospitals. In 1955, there had been 559,000 mentally ill people in hospitals; by the early 1960s it had plummeted to 90,000. But most families and communities were not prepared to work with these individuals who had been released. Funds were mismanaged and guidelines were vague. So where did the people go? Many are the homeless who now walk the streets. Dr. Torrey states that "there are as many individuals with schizophrenia homeless and living on the streets as there are in all hospitals. Many are victims of robbery, violence, and murder. Many end up in jails."

Today a large number of homeless people are mentally ill. Many of them are schizophrenic. Of those mentally ill people who are hospitalized, 40 percent are schizophrenic. Schizophrenia still accounts for a large percentage of all long-term hospitalizations.

The Brain, Chemistry, and Genetics

It is a glob of fat that weighs only about three pounds—that doesn't sound like much, nothing spectacular. However, the inner space of the brain holds more mystery than outer space. The brain is the most complex structure ever investigated by science. It is still a deep mystery, but its secrets are slowly being uncovered.

Brain 101

Have you ever looked inside your computer? The wiring found inside works well most of the time. Sometimes, though, your computer gets a glitch and crashes. Our brains are similar to the wiring of computers. Most of the time everything works well. Incoming perceptions are sent along appropriate signal paths and there is not a problem. But with schizophrenia, perceptions go along the wrong path or end up at the wrong destination.

The brain mediates all human behavior, so to understand some elements of mental illness, one must look at the brain and how it works. The brain contains about 100 billion nerve cells called neurons and many more supporting cells called glial cells. Glial cells are connecting tissues that bring in the nutrients that support neurons. While most organs have only a few different cell types, the brain has thousands of different kinds of neurons, each with a distinct chemistry, shape, and connection.

In some ways, the neuron is like all other cells and, in some ways, very different. It is like all cells in that it has a nucleus with chromosomes, a cell body, and a cell membrane, which lets materials in and out. The cell body, or cyton, encases the nucleus, which contains genetic material and energy-producing material.

Coming from one end of the cell body are the dendrites—structures that look like little trees. The Greek word *dendr* means "tree" and *ite* means "little." The dendrites receive the impulse or nerve message from the adjacent neuron. Dendrites come in many shapes and sizes, all relating to the way incoming messages are processed. The outgoing messages are carried along a long single branch called the axon, the path of the neuron that sends the signal to the next dendrite. A specialized structure on the end portion of the axon has packets of signaling chemicals called neurotransmitters.

Communication occurs at small, specialized gaps called the synapses. A synapse is actually the gap between two neurons. It is very important that these brain cells be able to communicate with each other. The usual form of communication involves electrical signals or impulses that travel to a neuron. Once a neuron is contacted, chemical signals occur that cross through the synapse. The chemical signals are translated into electrical signals. The electrical signals then move on to the next neuron and the process is repeated until all neurons are contacted.

These patterns of synapse connection are called the circuits of the brain. Large and small circuits make behavior and mental life possible. One of the mysteries of the brain is exactly how circuited neuronal activity gives rise to behavior and consciousness.

Structure of the Brain

The structure of the brain is also interesting. The cerebellum, or "little brain," controls balance and coordinates motion. The cerebrum has a region in the front part of the brain called the prefrontal cortex. The cerebrum is involved in the highest functions we perform. Beneath the cortex are enormous numbers of axons sheathed in an insulating substance called myelin. Other parts of the brain include the midbrain, the pons, and the medulla oblongata (which attaches to the spinal cord).

Gray matter is the cortex of the brain that contains nerve cells. Gray matter regions include the following structures:

⮑ **Basal ganglia.** The part of the brain involved in the initiation of motion. This is the area greatly affected by Parkinson's disease. It is also involved in the integration of motivational states and related to a group of addictive disorders.

⮑ **Amygdala.** This section is involved in the assignment of emotional meaning to events and objects. It also appears to play a special role in aversive or negative emotions such as fear.

⮑ **Hippocampus.** This area has the responsibility of initially encoding and consolidating explicit or episodic memories of persons, places, and things.

Overall, the organization of the brain at the cellular level involves many thousands of distinct neurons. These neurons integrate to form circuits for information processing, determined by their patterns of synaptic connections.

Chemistry 101

In addition to its complex structure, the brain is also a place of complex chemical activity. As we already learned, electrical signals are spurred into movement and transmission by molecules called neurotransmitters. There are two major kinds of neurotransmitters. The smaller neurotransmitters, called monoamines, are dopamine, serotonin, and norepinephrine. Larger molecules, which are essentially protein chains called peptides, include the opiate Substance P, and corticotropin-releasing factors (CRF). Glutamate is also a type of neurotransmitter and is currently being studied in order to verify its role in schizophrenia.

What Is a Neurotransmitter?

A neurotransmitter binds to the transmitter receptor and causes messages to be sent. There appear to be more than 100 different neurotransmitters. Although there are many kinds of receptors with many different signaling functions, we can divide most receptors into two general classes. One class is called a ligand-gated channel. The word "ligand" means "bind." So a ligand is a molecule, such as a neurotransmitter, that grabs onto a receptor. You might think of it as a piece of a puzzle that fits exactly into another piece.

Neurotransmitters working with this receptor open up a pore within the receptor molecule so electrical charges can enter the cell. The entry of positive charges may activate additional channels that let more positive charges enter. This causes the cell to release the neurotransmitter. The term used by scientists to describe this type of action in the neurotransmitter is "excitatory neurotransmitter receptors."

The second way a neurotransmitter acts is by letting negative charges into the cell, which keep the cell from firing. Most of the neurotransmitters in the brain, such as dopamine and serotonin, do not excite or inhibit, but act to produce complex biochemical changes in the receiving cells. Their receptors do not have pores, but interact with signaling proteins called G proteins that are inside the cell membrane.

Dopamine

In 1963, Swedish doctor Arvid Carlsson looked at the neurotransmitter dopamine and zeroed in on how chlorpromazine (Thorazine) works. He found that this drug blocked the flow of dopamine to the brain.

Dopamine is a neurotransmitter that acts to produce complex biochemical circuits. Too much of this neurotransmitter is a major cause of psychotic disorders. These neurotransmitters and their receptors are the targets of medications, such as antipsychotic drugs, that treat mental disorders.

Dopamine begins in the brain stem in clumps of a hundred million cells that are less than the size of one grain of sand. However, very few cells actually produce dopamine. For example, out of the brain's hundred billion neurons, only about 500,000 produce dopamine. The cell bodies of the dopamine neurons are clustered in regions of the midbrain, which is a section of the brain stem. When a person has too much dopamine, he or she may hear voices, but when there is too little, a condition known as Parkinson's disease occurs. Research on dopamine has revealed that there are five types of receptors: D1, D2, D3, D4, D5.

Serotonin

Serotonin is made up of a small number of neurons, and each sends its axons throughout the brain. A small number of neurons influence almost the entire brain. Serotonin is responsible for our brain's states, such as degree of arousal, ability to pay attention, and emotion.

In 1994, Dr. Paul Janssen of Johnson & Johnson found a new class of compounds that block both dopamine and serotonin in the brain. In chapter 6, we discussed these atypical antipsychotics. Dr. Janssen's discovery will most likely increase our chances of finding a cure for schizophrenia.

The Changing Brain

Another point about the brain is its plasticity, or ability to change. For example, every time you learn something new, the experience alters the structure of your brain. Right now you are reading and changing your brain. Scientists are just now learning about the structure and functions of the brain.

It takes 50,000 or 60,000 genes to build the brain, and it may have 100 trillion or a quadrillion synapses. Obviously, we are dealing with a very complex part of the body, and it is this fundamental realization that is beginning to lead to a greater understanding of how to treat mental disorders.

Genetics 101

Looking at schizophrenia is also of interest to geneticists because they want to know if schizophrenia is inherited. So far, studies have shown that it is. Parents, brothers, and sisters develop the condition on average ten times more than members of the general population. Children with a parent who is schizophrenic have a 15 percent chance of becoming schizophrenic. A large family study in Iowa showed the risk to brothers and sisters of schizophrenics stands at about 3 percent.

Studies of twins, both identical and fraternal, are of great interest to geneticists because they prove that the cause of schizophrenia lies in the genetic code. If both twins have schizophrenia, they are said to be concordant, whereas if only one has the illness they are described as discordant. The percent of concordant to the total is called the concordant rate. The concordance rate is 53 percent among identical twins and 15 percent among fraternal twins. This identifies the existence of a hereditary component, but because the concordance rate is not 100 percent, there must be other causal factors.

An interesting study in Denmark focused on 5,500 children separated at birth from parents during the years 1923 to 1947. The study found that 21 percent of the children who had schizophrenic parents later developed schizophrenia or a related illness, whereas only 11 percent who had nonschizophrenic parents later developed a mental illness. Children of parents with schizophrenia, even if they were adopted at birth, are more likely to manifest symptoms.

New technologies called DNA analysis have enabled scientists to look for pieces of the genetic code that may be affected by schizophrenia. While looking for genetic markers, two scientists at the University of British Columbia found an abnormality in a particular chromosome, labeled chromosome 5. Also, a number of British and Icelandic families with a generational history of schizophrenia yielded a chromosome 5 fragment.

A number of genetic factors may exist for schizophrenia that interact with one another or the environment, but nothing has been confirmed. However, efforts are under way to find genetic markers through analysis. Anne Pulver of Johns Hopkins Medical Center found a suspicious region on chromosome 22 that might be linked to schizophrenia, and another on chromosome 6. But as you can see, researchers are still in the beginning stages of identifying the precise location of the gene(s) that causes schizophrenia.

Current Brain Research

In researching how cells interact with genes in relation to the stimuli that cells experience, one study shows that certain cells of people with schizophrenia have a defect in how they relate to stimuli in the environment. Genes may put cells at risk for not developing the appropriate relationships as they mature.

How Do Scientists Study Brain Function?

↪ **MRI.** Magnetic resonance imaging takes pictures of the brain to show how it looks.

↪ **PET scans.** Positive emission tomography captures the activities and functions of the brain. Studies of PET scans compared the blood flow of people with schizophrenia who hear voices to those who do not hear voices. They found that those who hear voices have failed activity in two or more areas of the brain.

↪ **CT scans.** Computerized tomography magnifies areas of the brain; in particular, recent research has concentrated on enlarged ventricles.

↪ **MRSI.** Magnetic resonance spectroscopic imaging is a technology that looks at living brain tissue.

Below you will find other developments that are helping us to learn more about schizophrenia.

- Imaging has brought schizophrenia research into the mainstream of neuroscience.

- Scans on identical twins in which one has schizophrenia and the other one does not reveal that brain cavities called ventricles are slightly smaller in the normal twin.

- Imaging shows the thalamus, a control center for routing signals, is smaller than normal in the brains of schizophrenic patients.

- Scans have shown several brain regions to be highly active during hallucinations.

- Hearing false voices activates parts of the brain normally used in understanding speech.

- Visual hallucinations activate the thalamus.

- The regions of the brain that recognize sounds are underactive in schizophrenic patients.

- In autopsies, the area of the brain that regulates emotion, called the cingulate cortex, has been shown to be abnormal in schizophrenic patients.

Looking After Yourself

As we discussed in earlier chapters, schizophrenia is a family affair because if someone in your family has the condition, it is going to affect your life. Whether you are concerned or disturbed by the behavior, you are going to be involved. Hopefully, after reading this far, you will choose to be a supportive sibling or friend. Yet you should also keep in mind that being supportive and understanding is going to be a large commitment. Since you now know more about schizophrenia, you can understand why you will have to be persevering. One day the person may be the fun-loving individual you have always known, the next day, or even the next minute, he or she may be having an episode. However, as you also now know, this is not how it will always be; new medications and therapies have increased the chances of a schizophrenic leading a life free of symptoms.

Jim had been hospitalized and put on medication for negative symptoms of schizophrenia. He was released from the hospital after a week and he moved back in with his mother and two sisters.

At home, everyone was expected to pitch in and help with chores. Jim's task was to set the table for dinner and do the laundry, which he did at first. After a week, though, he just stopped bothering. Hoping the situation was temporary, Caly, his older sister, began to set the table for him so he wouldn't get in trouble. One day, as Caly was setting the table, Jim walked by and pushed her.

"Look, I'm doing this to be nice since you're such a lazy bum. You don't do anything."

Jim did not answer.

Belinda, Jim's younger sister, heard Caly and chimed in, "She's right. I'm sick of being your laundry servant."

Jim still did not answer.

Obviously, this family is having communication problems. Perhaps it would have been better if Caly and Belinda had tried to talk to Jim before they started doing his chores for him. If that didn't work, they could have gone to their mom.

Parents of a person with schizophrenia often feel torn between loyalties to the ill person and to other family members. Brothers and sisters often feel they are being cheated out of parental attention or finances. Caring for a relative with a prolonged illness can cause frustration, tension, anger, and sadness in a family.

My sister Maria is mentally ill. She is thirty years old now and was first hospitalized over twelve years ago, when she was diagnosed as having schizophrenia. She has not worked for all of these years and has been supported by my mother.

I am much younger than she is, and as a teenager I tried to ignore how different she really was. I went away to college as far as I possibly could and never went home unless I had to. I did keep in touch by telephone. It was only by taking myself out of the situation that I could survive. Mom was happy that I was so independent, but I always had mixed feelings of guilt and fear. I worried about what would happen if Mom died. I don't think I want to be the one who has to take care of my sister.

Shame and Blame

When a family member has schizophrenia, usually there is a search for someone to blame. Parents worry. Sisters and brothers have fears. Everyone's life is thrown upside down. It must be remembered that no one can make the problem go away, not even the person who is ill. At times, when people are frustrated, it is almost as if they can no longer understand that the mentally ill member of their family is not behaving this way on purpose. No one would really opt to be schizophrenic, just as no one would choose to get cancer. However, no matter how many times you remind yourself of this, you will still go through the following emotions:

- **Bitterness.** Why did this have to happen to us?

- **Blame.** What did we do wrong?

- **Shame.** What will people think of us?

- **Blaming each other.** If you had only been a better parent.

- **Anger.** Why should I give this ill member of the family all of my attention? He doesn't deserve it.

- **Total denial.** There is nothing wrong with this girl, she just needs to pull herself together.

- **Sorrow.** I feel I have lost my brother or sister.

- **Fear.** Will the ill person harm himself or others?

- **Ambivalence.** We love him a lot, but we wish he would just go away.

- **Depression.** We can't talk without crying.

- **Excessive searching.** Was it something we did to him?

Be Good to Yourself

Self-care is critical for every member of the family. Let go of guilt and shame. Remember, the illness is not the result of poor parenting or being a bad sister or brother. Likewise, it is not a personal failure of the individual. For most people, the times in which coping is most difficult is at the onset of the illness, during adolescence, and during episodes when the person behaves in ways that are unpredictable and unacceptable.

While the community offers support groups, the families of people with schizophrenia are the main source of support. Below you will find ways to keep yourself and your outlook healthy so that you can continue to be supportive.

- **Value your own privacy.** Keep your friendships and outside interests. Continue to do things and be involved in your own activities, whether it is sports or club activities.

- **Keep your life as organized as possible.** Value your own physical and mental health by getting enough sleep, exercise, and nutrition.

⮑ **Spend time with other family members**. As a brother or sister, you may share some of the same guilt as your parents. You may secretly worry about becoming ill, too, or think about your parents' getting sick and leaving you to care for your ill relative. Spend time with other family members and share your fears and worries.

⮑ **Accept the limits of what you can do.** Understand that you cannot fix all of the problems that arise because your sibling is ill. Allow your parents to deal with the stress, too.

⮑ **Budget your money and spending.** Depending upon the family budget, medical expenses can drain the financial resources of a family. Talk with your parents about how they are doing financially and find out how much of an impact the expenses will have upon your life.

Some Dos and Don'ts for Helping a Person

Having a parent or sibling with a mental illness often impacts the image of one's family and can affect emotional well-being. However, schizophrenia is an illness in which acceptance is half the battle. Although feeling ashamed of your relative is a common response, it is not a healthy one. Your life and your loved one's recovery will be much smoother if you can be a supportive friend or sibling or child. So work at maintaining your best mental health because it is through caring for yourself that you will be able to help the ill person.

85

Defy the Illness

We have talked about knowing the condition and educating yourself about specific symptoms. You will find tips below that will allow your life with a mentally ill person to be less traumatic.

- **Keep the message simple.** Be as straightforward and as honest as possible.

- **Concern must be constructive.** Try not to show overt anxiety or distress and avoid harsh or direct criticism.

- **Point out areas of concern.** Explore how you can face difficulties together, but do not try to control the person's life.

- **Have realistic expectations.** Accept failures as a good try, and compliment achieved goals.

- **Maintain links with professional services.** If things are not working out at home, consider alternatives by acknowledging when it is time to let go.

Recognizing Relapse

Learning to note signs of relapse, like any marked change in behavior such as eating, sleeping, or other habits, is one of the most important skills that you can work on developing. If the ill person begins to exhibit excessive emotions, inappropriate behavior, or difficulty in carrying out usual activities, notify the doctor and ask for an evaluation of his or her medications. Have a crisis plan ready, with emergency telephone numbers and procedures in mind.

Legal and Ethical Issues

Sometimes family members have a difficult time understanding the legal and ethical issues of confidentiality. They think they should be told everything that has been discussed between doctor and patient. The caregiver can receive information about signs and symptoms, expected course of the illness, treatment strategies, and signs of possible relapse. But at times, caregivers think that if they do not know every detail about what has been said in therapy, they cannot be as helpful. However, confidentiality is the law.

In 1996, the Supreme Court ruled in the case of *Jaffee vs. Redmon* that a psychotherapist has privilege in federal court. Privilege means the doctor does not have to reveal conversations with or information about the client. This is to protect the best interests of the person. If the doctor wants to reveal any information, the patient must sign a release granting the physician permission.

What Are Other Legal Questions?

The issue of civil rights enters into any attempt to provide treatment. Laws protecting patients from involuntary commitment have become very strict, and families and community organizations may become frustrated in their efforts to see that a severely mentally ill individual gets needed help.

Although laws vary from state to state, generally when people are dangerous to themselves or others because of a mental disorder, the police can assist in getting an emergency psychiatric evaluation and commitment.

Managing Day to Day

As you know, for many years there was a pessimistic myth—even among professionals—that all was hopeless after a person was diagnosed with schizophrenia. Today, people working with schizophrenics are more optimistic, but they insist that rehabilitation begins from day one. Even with people who have battled the condition for a long time, professionals still hold hope for recovery. Researchers say that the hope for recovery from schizophrenia is about the same as recovery from heart disease. Your family can be part of this optimism by giving encouragement to the ill person on a day-to-day basis.

How Can You Be Sure Medication Is Taken?

Try organizing medications with medication calendars or pillboxes that are marked with each day. At the beginning of the week, put the pills in the appropriate compartments, and then check to see if the medication has been taken each day. These small boxes can be purchased at a pharmacy.

You can also purchase an electronic timer that beeps when medications should be taken. Another idea is to investigate injectable medications that need to be injected only once a week. There are also indirect factors that can influence a schizophrenic's decision to take his or her medication:

- ⇔ **Reduce stress.** People with schizophrenia have problems with lots of sensory stimulation. For example, lots of things going on causes sensory overload. Reduce stress by keeping routines simple. Plan nonstressful, low-key daily activities but keep big events to a minimum.

- ⇔ **Be consistent.** Caregivers should agree on a plan of action and follow-up. This reduces confusion and stress for the person who is ill.

⇨ **Maintain peace and calm at home.** Depending on the personalities in the home, this may be a big order. Try to speak one at a time and at a reasonably moderate pace. Also, use shorter sentences.

⇨ **Be supportive and positive.** Being positive instead of critical will help in the long run. People with schizophrenia need lots of encouragement because their self-esteem is often very fragile. This illness undermines a person's confidence, initiative, patience, and memory.

⇨ **Help the ill person set realistic goals.** People with schizophrenia need encouragement to regain their former skills and interests. They may also want to try new things.

⇨ **Gradually increase independence.** As they participate in tasks and activities, help them seek independence. However, set limits on how much abnormal behavior is acceptable.

⇨ **Learn to cope with stress constructively.** You will need to be a positive role model in handling stress so that your family members can learn from your example.

Are People with Schizophrenia Likely to Be Violent?

Most schizophrenics are not violent and typically are withdrawn and prefer to be left alone. The figure of the "violent madman" is prevalent in movies and books, but this is a myth. Although news and movies often link mental illness to criminal violence, studies indicate that except for those who had a criminal record before the onset of the illness, most schizophrenics do not become violent after diagnosis. When violent incidents do occur, they usually get a tremendous amount of publicity, which is what supports the perception that all schizophrenics are violent.

Most often, schizophrenic violence stems from hearing voices that tell the person to target a particular group of people. Many mass or serial killers have worked under what they consider to be a mandate from the voice of "God." Persons who are paranoid and have stopped taking their medication are more at risk for violent behavior.

Overall, people with schizophrenia are less violent than others. Many of them are so passive they have little conflict with anyone and prefer to be left alone so they will not have to interact. One study showed that out of all murders committed, only about 2 percent are by people diagnosed with schizophrenia.

Are Suicide Threats Real?

In 1994, a Finnish study found that many patients who committed suicide saw their psychiatrists as recently as ten days before their attempt, but did not mention their intention. Many people with schizophrenia attempt suicide but do not succeed. Suicide is a serious danger to people with schizophrenia. If the person threatens or tries to commit suicide, get help immediately. About 15 percent of people with schizophrenia commit suicide, and young adult males are at especially high risk.

James was a brilliant college student under psychiatric care for psychosis. He had been taking tranquilizers, but one day he finished the bottle by taking forty times the prescribed dose. He put on his shoes, walked to the college clinic, and had his stomach pumped. He later tried to strangle himself with a sheet. Fortunately, he was saved just in time on both occasions.

Suicide attempts often lead to the first encounter with psychiatric services, and they are also frequently the cause of repeated hospitalization. Out of all the people with schizophrenia, it is thought that at least 30 percent attempt suicide. This figure is disturbingly high, so you must never take any threat of suicide lightly.

Future Challenges

Looking ahead to the future of treatment of mental illness, there are major challenges to be tackled. Trends in the last twenty-five years include:

- ➥ Extraordinary growth of scientific research on the brain and behavior

- ➥ Introduction of new treatments and imaging tools

- ➥ A shift in society's approaches to organization and financing of mental health care

- ➥ Emergence of powerful consumer and family advocacy movements

Although these trends should continue, there are many other challenges that can now be focused upon. Let's look at eight super-challenges that we can meet in the next few years.

Challenge Number One: Realization that Schizophrenia Is an Illness

Schizophrenia is a disease. All behavior and symptoms of schizophrenia originate in the brain. Physical changes in the brain often cause changes in other parts of the body. For example, a nightmare is a mental state caused by changes in the brain that can cause a racing heart or dry mouth.

In the future you can expect to see the term "somatic health" used instead of "physical health." "Somatic" means pertaining to the body. Also, as recent trends in treatment involve both mind and body medicine, expect to see even more integration in these two areas in the coming years.

Schizophrenia steals the lives of young people at a time when important decisions about life are being made. Therefore, it is imperative that our national interests concentrate on helping people who have mental illness. Even though a staggering $17 billion per year is spent on caring for schizophrenia patients, it is still not enough.

Challenge Number Two: More Education

Ignorance about mental illness is everywhere. Very few people know much about it. Can you help? Absolutely. You can correct misinformation.

Many school systems now require service projects as a requirement to graduate. This could be your opportunity to design a project to help people with schizophrenia. You can work with support groups like NAMI or ask to speak to groups about the condition.

Challenge Number Three: Organize or Volunteer at a Support Group

It was November 1978, on a cold blustery day in Madison, Wisconsin, when two women met to talk about how helpless and alone they felt. Both had sons with schizophrenia. After a long discussion, they reasoned that since they felt so much better after talking to each other, they should give other people the opportunity to share their feelings. On this day, the National Alliance for the Mentally Ill (NAMI) was established. On September 7, 1979, 268 delegates met for their first meeting and the AMI was born.

Although the idea of support groups is old, the help and support they provide is timeless. In 1864, John Thomas Perceval formed the Alleged Lunatics of Friends Society in London. Perceval, a nobleman and son of a former prime minister, was hospitalized for three years because of hallucinations. After his release, he spent twenty years exposing negligence and violations in hospitals for the mentally ill.

Dear Dr. Martinez,

I appreciate your suggestion that I try to learn more about schizophrenia by reading and volunteering at the National Alliance for the Mentally Ill (NAMI). I called the facilitator and she invited me to participate. There are two groups in this chapter of NAMI, one for family members and one for the clients.

I told Jason what I was going to do and he asked to come along. I was so surprised. You were right, he is very curious about how other people deal with having schizophrenia.

At the meeting there were several college graduates and even an attorney. The facilitator asked the group to talk about their experiences with schizophrenia. It seemed that everyone shared a bond because they had such an understanding of each other.

After we left the meeting, Jason thanked me for taking him and told me that he felt a lot better than he had before.

Lisa

Challenge Number Four: Decrease the Stigma of Mental Illness

You can help overcome the stigma that surrounds mental illness. Stigma is shown in bias, stereotyping, distrust, fear, embarrassment, anger, or avoidance of people because they have schizophrenia. Stigma also leads others to treat schizophrenics as less than equal and not to hire or even befriend them. Such treatment reduces the schizophrenic's opportunities, self-esteem, and dignity while elevating their feelings of isolation and hopelessness. Stigma leads to discrimination and abuse.

Challenge Number Five: Give People the Facts About Mental Illness and Violence

The likelihood that a schizophrenic will be violent is low, except when he or she has a dual disorder or an addiction like substance abuse. This is why we need to work on schizophrenics receiving the proper treatment. If schizophrenics receive treatment, they are less likely to be addicted to drugs, and, therefore, less likely to be violent. If our national goal was to help those with mental disorders and if it was pursued by more people, violence would be decreased.

Challenge Number Six: Scientific Research Must Continue

Mental disorders are diagnosed by symptoms, signs, and functional impairment. Neuroscience will continue to expand as more and more is found out about the complex chemistry of the brain. Recognizing schizophrenia as a neurological brain disease is important because this recognition will influence the study of imaging techniques. Hopefully, this will create even more interest and funding so that research can become even more refined.

Genetics and molecular biology are also going to be growing fields of research. More knowledge means new treatments with fewer side effects. Expect new pharmacological agents and psychotherapies for the treatment of schizophrenia and other mental disorders.

Challenge Number Seven: Public Awareness Is Essential

Project Hope is an assistance program located in central Florida that is dedicated to helping the homeless. According to the nurses and physicians working at this project, more than half of the people they deal with have schizophrenia.

You can help by participating in campaigns that teach people about mental illness. Remember, people who are not affected by mental illness often have the most misinformation about it. You can also work to help the homeless, not just by getting them off the street but also by enabling them to be diagnosed and treated. Building shelters is not enough. Community facilities must also offer treatment.

Challenge Number Eight: Funding for Services Must Be Expanded

The mental health profession is generally considered the stepchild of funding. Encourage more money for services. As stated by the National Advisory Mental Health Council in 1998, "New strategies must be devised to bridge the gap between research and practice." Additionally, if you look at research dollars spent on mental illness compared to other illnesses, the amount is much smaller.

Schizophrenia is hard for everyone to deal with. Undoubtedly, the diagnosed person, family, and friends will struggle as life goes on and everyone is learning to cope. Remember, though, schizophrenia is an illness that can be treated. Life will get better. Remember, too, that if more people become proactive and organized, all of the super-challenges we just discussed may become reality. Can you help? Yes, you can, and now you know the ways in which to do this.

Glossary

affective disorder   Mental illness characterized by great swings in emotion, also known as mood disorder.

anecdotal records   Diary or record of daily happenings and behaviors that should be kept during treatment.

antipsychotics   Family of drugs that act to reduce the symptoms of psychotic conditions.

atypical antipsychotics   Newer, more advanced version of antipsychotic drugs that decrease the symptoms of a mental illness.

bipolar disorder   Periodic, recurrent mood disorder with periods of complete normalcy, not to be confused with schizophrenia.

blunted emotions   Absence of reaction, emotion, or response.

delusion   Pathologically derived error of belief held with unshakable conviction that cannot be corrected with logical proof.

dementia praecox   Outdated term that once defined schizophrenia.

dendrites   Treelike structures that receive the impulse or nerve message from adjacent neurons.

glial cells Connecting tissues found in the central nervous system that bring in the nutrients that support neurons in their work.

hallucination Perceived sensation with no external basis.

moral management Outdated form of treating mental illness in which delusions were thought to be cured by producing creative distractions.

neuroleptics Family of drugs with antipsychotic reactions.

neurons Cells with specialized processes; the fundamental function unit of all brain activity.

psychosis General term for a number of major psychiatric illnesses in which mental experiences are qualitatively different from the normal range of experience.

relapse To slip back into a former state, such as experiencing episodes of paranoia.

schizophrenia Illness that stems from the brain that interferes with a person's ability to think, feel, and act.

stigma Mark of shame or discredit that is attributed to the mentally ill.

synapses Small, specialized gaps where communication occurs between neurons.

tardive dyskinesia Syndrome of involuntary movements especially around the mouth associated with long-term antipsychotic drug treatment.

thought disorder Symptom of schizophrenia where thinking and speech become difficult.

withdrawal Process of removing oneself from society and relationships with others.

Where to Go for Help

In the United States

National Alliance for Research on Schizophrenia and
Depression (NARSAD)
60 Cutter Mill Road, Suite 404
Great Neck, NY 11021
(516) 829-0091
Web site: http://www.mhsource.com/narsad

National Alliance for the Mentally Ill (NAMI)
Colonial Place Three
2107 Wilson Boulevard, Suite 300
Arlington, VA 22201-3042
(800) 950-NAMI (6264)
Web site: http://www.nami.org

National Institute of Mental Health (NIMH)
Public Inquiries
6001 Executive Boulevard, Room 8184, MSC 9663
Bethesda, MD 20892-9663
(301) 443-4513
Web site: http://www.nimh.nih.gov

National Mental Health Association (NMHA)
1021 Prince Street
Alexandria, VA 22314-2971
(800) 969-6642
Web site: http://www.nmha.org

National Mental Health Consumers' Self-Help
    Clearinghouse
1211 Chestnut Street, Suite 1207
Philadelphia, PA 19107
(800) 553-4539
Web site: http://www.mhselfhelp.org

In Canada

Canadian Psychiatric Association
260-441 MacLaren Street
Ottawa, ON K2P 2H3
(613) 234-2815
e-mail: cpa@cpa-apc.org
Web site: http://www.cpa.ca

Canadian Psychological Association
151 Slater Street, Suite 205
Ottawa, ON K1P 5H3
e-mail: cpa@cpa.ca
Web site: http://www.cpa.org

Schizophrenia Society of Canada
75 The Donway West, Suite 814
Don Mills, ON M3C 2E9
(800) 809-HOPE (4673)
Web site: http://www.schizophrenia.ca

Web Sites

HealthlinkUSA
www.healthlinkusa.com

MentalWellness.com
www.mentalwellness.com

Schizophrenia.com
www.schizophrenia.com

Schizophrenia-Help Online Resource Center
www.schizophrenia-help.com

Schizophrenia Knowledge Center
www.schizophrenianet.org

For Further Reading

Adamec, Christine. *How to Live with a Mentally Ill Person.* New York: John Wiley & Sons, 1996.

Andreasen, Nancy C., ed. *Schizophrenia: From Mind to Molecule.* Washington, DC: American Psychiatric Press, 1994.

Keefe, Richard S. E., and Philip D. Harvey. *Understanding Schizophrenia: A Guide to the New Research on Causes and Treatment.* New York: The Free Press, 1994.

Marsh, Diane T., and Rex Dickens. *How to Cope with Mental Illness in Your Family.* New York: Putnam Publishing, 1998.

Noll, Richard. *The Encyclopedia of Schizophrenia and the Psychotic Disorders.* New York: Facts on File, 1992.

Torrey, E. Fuller. *Surviving Schizophrenia.* (3rd ed.) New York: HarperCollins, 1995.

Tsuang, Ming T., and Stephen V. Faraone. *Schizophrenia: The Facts.* New York: Oxford University Press, 1997.

Wyden, Peter. *Conquering Schizophrenia: A Father, His Son, and a Medical Breakthrough.* New York: Alfred A. Knopf, 1998.

Index